I0819658

A VOICE LIKE MINE

A VOICE LIKE MINE

A Memoir

DEB HAALAND

HENRY HOLT AND COMPANY
NEW YORK

Henry Holt and Company
Publishers since 1866
120 Broadway
New York, New York 10271
www.henryholt.com

Henry Holt® and Ⓗ® are registered trademarks of
Macmillan Publishing Group, LLC.
EU Representative: Macmillan Publishers Ireland Ltd.,
1st Floor, The Liffey Trust Centre,
117–126 Sheriff Street Upper, Dublin 1, D01 YC43

Distributed in Canada by Raincoast Book Distribution Limited

Library of Congress Cataloging-in-Publication Data

Names: Haaland, Debra A., 1960– author.
Title: A voice like mine : a memoir / Deb Haaland.
Description: First edition. | New York : Henry Holt and Company, 2026.
Identifiers: LCCN 2025051404 | ISBN 9781250434227 (hardcover) | ISBN 9781250434234 (ebook)
Subjects: LCSH: Haaland, Debra A., 1960– | Indian legislators—United States | Women legislators—United States | United States. Congress. House | United States. Department of the Interior—Officials and employees | Women cabinet officers—United States | Cabinet officers—United States | Pueblo women—New Mexico | Pueblo Indians—New Mexico | LCGFT: Autobiographies
Classification: LCC E901.1.H33 A3 2026
LC record available at https://lccn.loc.gov/2025051404

First Edition 2026

Designed by Omar Chapa

Printed in the United States of America

10 9 8 7 6 5 4 3 2 1

For those who have never given up

CONTENTS

A VOICE LIKE MINE

PROLOGUE

Coming Home

On January 18, 2025, I returned to Albuquerque by myself for the first time in four years. Winter had come to the high desert, and as my plane lowered toward the runway, I saw bare trees and blades of brown desert grass bending to the wind. The Sandia Mountains looked grand in the midday sun. *Sandía* means "watermelon" in Spanish, so named because our granite mountains glow pink at sunset. Before the granite rose from magma, this land was a shallow marine basin, and you can still find clamshell fossils when hiking the Sandia Crest. These mountains east of Albuquerque have always helped me keep my bearings. Each rising sun offers an opportunity for progress.

I thought about the many times I had hiked to the Sandia Crest and about the smell of pine needles and crisp air, miles from any car exhaust. From the top, Albuquerque looks tidy, its main streets laid out on a neat grid; beyond it, open space stretches into the distance. The city's growth is contained by the Sandia Mountains' designation as a national forest to the east and by Indian pueblos to the south, west, and north. The pueblos here do what they do best: conserve the land. That week in January, temperatures dropped below the teens, reinforcing my sense that the work we had done to address the climate crisis while I led the US Interior Department was more urgent than ever.

There was a calamitous chill beyond the unseasonable air. In a few days, Donald Trump would be sworn in for a second term, and the country's fear and worry were palpable. Along with millions of Americans, I had done all I could to elicit a different result. My desire to defend my community and the people of New Mexico grew as I walked through the Albuquerque Sunport, the wheels of my carry-on clicking away on the terminal's brick floors. For the first time in four years, I was free to say and do as I pleased without the constraints of being a federal employee. I could feel in my entire body that this fight was personal.

As interior secretary, I was charged with upholding the United States' trust and treaty obligations to our 574 federally recognized tribes, overseeing the stewardship of more than five hundred million acres of public lands, shepherding the research and scientific knowledge painstakingly collected by dedicated federal employees, and seeing to it that our cultural heritage was protected for future generations. But the mission as written doesn't capture my emotional attachment to the beautiful landscapes and sacred places I visited when I led the agency or my devotion to the people with whom I worked. Federal civil service employees worldwide understand the importance of America leading with an eye toward the betterment of humanity and the conservation of our planet's resources and gifts. Trump's reelection jeopardized these fundamental goals; our forty-seventh president's dual purposes are to disassemble our government and burn our planet for profit.

I joined President Joe Biden's cabinet as the daughter of a federal civil servant and a US marine who had served in Vietnam and as a sober alcoholic; a single mother; a cook, baker, and entrepreneur; a law school graduate; an organizer; an elected official; and a Pueblo woman.

Back in Albuquerque, I was starting over. My marriage was ending, and I wasn't sure I would ever return to the peaceful adobe house my second husband and I had filled with paintings and weavings from Indian country. Our house was in a quiet, pastoral neighborhood where I ran on trails beneath old cottonwood trees in the early mornings. Now I planned to run for governor of New Mexico. I felt a sense of urgency to fight for the folks whose voices had been silenced by the outcome of the 2024 election.

I began this memoir by reflecting on my Laguna Pueblo grandparents' powerful influence on my everyday life. Each day, I strive to emulate their values, perspectives, and indelible work ethic. Thinking about their ability to survive an oppressive Indian Boarding School gave me the courage to begin and finish the investigative reports on those schools that are among my proudest accomplishments as interior secretary. Listening to the testimony of countless survivors made me realize that the damage those schools wrought has continued to affect me in ways I had not considered before.

Unlike any previous interior secretary, I had inherited trauma caused by the very institution I led. But I had also inherited the courage, perseverance, and love of community that had been passed down to me since my Pueblo ancestors' first footsteps on the desert earth.

We all have obligations to our earth, our country, our communities, our families, and to each other as human beings. Beneath the desert sun, I shake off the chill and run, one step at a time.

PART I

ANCESTORS

THE MOST BEAUTIFUL SIGHT

Red rocks stand guard, as the eagle flies between
and near the hawk without touching
even the tips of his wings.
Eagle searches for a live morsel
to nourish his rightful body; the morsel
offers its life for beauty shimmering in sunlight.

I want to prepare his dinner. Make sure he is fed.
Give him a place, next to me.
Invite him back each day to our blue bowl of sky
to fly for my children and me to revere.

The most beautiful sight
is all my children in one place together.
Each doing his part to ensure happiness and comfort for the rest. We make sure the eagle has enough, that we take only what we need.

The eagle did his part to give a son to me.
I wrapped him in a colorful blanket, took him home. We sat in the shade beside the old cottonwood
under its crooked arms and young leaves dangling
like paper hearts on small bits of string.

A warm breeze made my touch welcome, and I told my son a few stories
of the old days
when eagles never hungered and fields were plentiful.
I pointed out the place where water ran freely, like the eagle.
I said I would take him there now.
He smiled and nodded his beautiful head.

I invite my children to sit with me. That is the world to me.
We sit together, breathing in.

CHAPTER 1

The Turquoise Clan

My mother always said I was born in the middle of a snowstorm. She had gone home to be with my grandparents in Winslow, Arizona, because the Marine Corps had shipped off my dad on a military mission somewhere, and she thought it would be good for her and my older sisters to spend time with her parents. Having given birth to my sisters Zoe, who was one year ahead of me, and Denise, who was one year ahead of Zoe, my mom knew when it was time to go to the hospital. My grandpa drove her there at four in the morning, his windshield wipers a-blazing.

The way my mom told the story, my grandfather was so caught up in the moment that he forgot to put on his trousers. He came in from starting the truck wearing his fedora, a winter coat, and his white flannel long johns. My mother told me she laughed despite her labor pains, and I imagine it must have been the genuine laugh that deepened the dimples in her cheeks and forced her eyes nearly shut. Grandpa looked down and went to retrieve his pants from the back of the house. I must have been born around six in the morning. My mother could not quite remember, and my birth certificate doesn't specify the time. Regardless, when my mother left the hospital with me, we returned to my grandparents' home.

I am an enrolled member of the Laguna Pueblo, and home to me is my grandmother's small rock house beneath the deep red sandstone mesa in the village of Mesita in central New Mexico. I know the whistle of the train below the village like the sound of my own voice. Any time of the year, cedar smoke from outdoor mud ovens lingers in the air as Pueblo women extend the legacy of their mothers through the methodical act of baking bread in traditional ovens.

In Keres, the language of the Laguna Pueblo people, my name means "Crushed Turquoise," and like my mother and grandmother, I belong to the Turquoise Clan. We are a matrilineal society, so at birth we take our mother's clan name, and we learn from the women in our families what it means to be Pueblo. For me, those women were Grandma Helen, Auntie Ann, and my mother, Mary Elizabeth, God rest all their souls.

My maternal grandmother, Helen Steele, came from the Laguna Pueblo, about forty miles west of Albuquerque. In my earliest memories of traveling from Albuquerque to Mesita Village, Route 66 was still a two-lane road. You had to cross a narrow metal truss bridge that traversed the Rio Puerco, where a Stuckey's travel store sat lonely in a gravel parking lot scattered with tufts of high desert grass and tumbleweed. We rarely, if ever, stopped at the Stuckey's, but when we passed it, I always imagined that my parents would buy me ice cream or candy, not the Indian trinkets it was known for, which reminded tourists they were in Indian country. The trinkets usually consisted of miniature teepees, cardboard drums, and colorful feather headdresses, although the Pueblo Indians live in rock houses and do not wear feather headdresses.

Laguna is one of the handful of Indian pueblos in New Mexico that survived the Spanish and US governments' attempts at colonization. At one time, hundreds of pueblos dotted New Mexico; today, just nineteen remain. The pueblos were once Spanish Land Grants, and today some of our neighbors are descended from the original Spanish families who came to New Mexico all those centuries ago. Our communities have lived next to each other for hundreds of years, and in many instances people from neighboring villages fell in love and married, mixing our Indian and Spanish blood.

Laguna has six distinct villages. Some are remote, but Route 66, which my grandma called "the road to California," runs past three of them, including Mesita. Compared to the red sandstone mesa atop gypsum hills to its north, Mesita is a little mesa made of basalt rock. To the west, Mount Taylor looms majestically. Once a mighty volcano, it gave rise and purpose to the lands where my ancestors built their first basalt walls after migrating to the Rio Grande Valley in the late 1200s from places like Chaco Canyon, Bears Ears, Mesa Verde, and other ancient Pueblo villages across the Southwest. Between the village and the big red mesa lie the Rio San Jose, the railroad tracks, and fields of fruit trees, corn, beans, squash, and chile.

My grandma told me that when the railroad tracks were being laid through Laguna land in the late 1800s, her grandmother and aunties sold the workers homemade sheep cheese and home-baked bread. They were some of the pueblo's first entrepreneurs. My grandma also spoke of her horse named John. After a paved road was built between Mesita and the village of Laguna, John pulled her and her father in a wagon along the smooth, new hardtop.

Laguna Pueblo became a waypoint for people moving west, especially during the Depression. Over the years, people would come through, down on their luck and looking for a better way of life in California, but the Lagunas never felt the Depression because they were farmers and still lived in a bartering economy with no cars, no house payments, and no utilities to speak of. Laguna would not move to a cash economy until the Jackpile Uranium Mine opened in 1950 near the village of Paguate. That mine operated for thirty years; with nine underground and three open-pit mines, it was one of the largest open-pit uranium operations in the world.

For many people, working at the Jackpile Mine was an opportunity to earn a solid paycheck while staying close to home. For others, it was a source of physical hardship and sickness. My cousin lost the hearing in one of his ears from the dynamite they blasted three times a day. Those blasts created the web of underground mines but also cracked the walls of many traditional rock homes in Paguate. During thirty years of dynamite blasts that gouged out vast pieces of land, Laguna's "progress" came with devastating trade-offs. After the mining company closed its doors and the earth movers and drilling rigs moved on, uranium tailings remained in every gust of wind. It would be more than two decades before the company began repairing the damage.

My maternal grandfather, Tony Toya, came from Jemez

Pueblo, which is north and west of Albuquerque. I always knew we were approaching Jemez by the deep red rock mesas in the distance. My grandfather's ancestors joined Jemez from Pecos Pueblo, now a National Historical Park, in 1838. To visit that pueblo is to realize that centuries ago, it was a thriving Indigenous community and a center of immense trade. The colonization of Pecos Pueblo began in the mid-1500s, and it ultimately forced my grandfather's ancestors to leave their land for good.

Because it was combined with Pecos Pueblo, Jemez has two Catholic feast days each year—August 2 for the Feast of Saint Persingula, the Catholic patron saint of Pecos, and November 12 for Saint Diego, the patron saint of Jemez. As the story goes, Spanish soldiers were pursuing a group of Jemez men one day in the summer of 1694 when they came to the edge of a mesa. The men had to choose between being captured by the Spanish soldiers or falling to their deaths. They decided to jump off the cliff, and as they did, an image of Saint Diego appeared on the cliff wall, and the men floated down to safety.

Each feast day, the people move in procession with the saint statues from the church and place them in a lavishly decorated shrine in the village plaza. Members of the pueblo dance and sing in honor of the Catholic saints. The women cook rich red and green chile stews, bake bread, make pans of Jemez enchiladas, and open their homes to all visitors. It's likely one of the few places in America where you can walk into the home of someone you've never met and sit down to a traditional Pueblo meal.

Even though we spent more of my childhood days at Mesita Village, some of my most cherished memories were made in Jemez. My great-grandfather Jose Ray Toya lived there in a small rock house close to the plaza. On feast days, we would visit him before things accelerated. Great-grandpa Toya had long black hair that he wore in a ponytail. Sometimes he would let me brush his hair with a hairbrush the circumference of a juice glass that he'd made from many strands of straw bound together with a strip of leather.

When we worked in his cornfield together, Grandpa Toya would talk about the rain and why we pray for it. Watching water from the irrigation ditch fill the rows of corn was like watching a miracle unfold. I didn't quite make the connection between the water in my grandfather's field and our traditional ceremonies, but I eventually realized how our songs and dances contributed to the natural cycles and the blessings we received from the earth.

One Saturday early in the morning, my mom packed us all into our black-and-white Buick station wagon for a dance on the Hopi reservation. My grandma called out from the front door for my mom to take the umbrellas. My mother looked up at the sky and replied, "It isn't going to rain."

We arrived at one of the mesa-top villages on the Hopi Reservation and put out the folding chairs and stools my mom had brought. Then we all sat watching the dancers and singers beseech the sky for rain. It isn't easy for a young child to sit for hours, sometimes under the hot sun, as an observer with no active role other than to take in the blessings of ceremonial activity, but I learned patience early, and it has stayed with me.

On that day, it seemed that every observer was there for the same purpose: to pray in unison for the rain that corn needs to grow and thrive in summertime in the desert Southwest.

Thick black clouds soon darkened the wide, clear blue sky we'd traveled under, and it began to rain. It rained harder than I had ever felt, and by the time we splashed back to the car on the top of that giant rock, we were soaked with the blessings of Creator. On the way down the mesa, with the rain outpacing our windshield wipers, I saw the grandest waterfalls pouring off the sides of all the mesas we passed. My sisters and I were quiet, almost in disbelief, until my sister Zoe cried out, "*Mah-me Koch!*" which roughly translates to "Boy! It sure is raining!" My mother laughed, and we all joined her, reveling in the joy of a summer downpour in the high desert.

In Mesita, I would spend hours and hours in the desert, at the river, and climbing the enormous red mesa. My cousins and I hiked almost daily. We could have encountered rattlesnakes or any other danger, but we were kids out to explore the desert. Once, on our way home from the top of the mesa, my cousin Terence got caught in quicksand at the river. We pulled him out with sticks, entirely failing to understand the urgency of the challenge.

Terence and his brother, Paully, were gifted athletes who ran and played baseball through every phase of school. Sometimes, when we were driving here or there with their dad, my uncle Paul, Terence and Paully would challenge each other to a foot-race. Uncle Paul would stop the car, and the boys would get out and run to my grandma's house, my uncle and I cheering them on through the open car window. Although I was inspired at the time, I didn't start running until I was forty.

I was born into a culture that requires me to give myself over to many obligations. Being Native American is difficult.

Once you begin a ceremony, you can't quit until it's finished, even if it takes several days. The work isn't done until the last pot is washed and the floor swept. As a result, I was a teenager when I learned to go without sleep. This has served me well in every campaign job I've ever had.

I came into the world as a descendant of the first inhabitants of the North American continent and as the daughter of an immigrant family. My dad is a third-generation Norwegian American, and my middle name is Anne, meant to be pronounced ANN-ah, after my Norwegian great-grandmother. Both that and my last name, Haaland (originally spelled Håland), were Americanized when my Norwegian forebears immigrated to the United States in the late 1800s.

I didn't grow up debating politics at the dinner table or interning at my dad's office; my parents never took me to rallies or speeches. I didn't even know they were Republicans until I started paying attention and voting myself. But I watched them wake up every morning to serve our country, regardless of who worked in the White House, and I knew no other way.

The beauty of working from the ground up is the experience you gain along the way. As your experience builds, it gets easier to know how to instruct and, thus, to lead. I led by example. I learned that from my family—from my father's marine career and from my mother's Pueblo culture. I wouldn't be who I am today without the people who raised me.

CHAPTER 2

"Kill the Indian"

My grandmother told me that her father was the first in her family to be sent to an Indian Boarding School. The schools were part of the US government's policy of forcing Indigenous children to leave their families and cultures to "kill the Indian in him, but save the man," as army officer Richard Henry Pratt, who founded the Carlisle Indian School, put it in 1892. Grandma said that her dad was put on a train as a child and sent east to Carlisle, the first Native American boarding school in the United States. When my great-grandfather came home, the school administrators had given him a new name: Gaylord Steele.

My mother often repeated that story, so I grew up believing it. Much later, I searched for "Gaylord Steele" in the Carlisle Indian School Digital Resource Center at Dickinson College. Dickinson is in Carlisle, Pennsylvania, about a mile and a half from the site of the Carlisle Indian School, where the US Army War College now stands. Because of its proximity to the school site, and with the help of Native Americans who wanted to ensure that Carlisle's students were not forgotten,

Dickinson created the digital archive, which continues to grow. But I never found "Gaylord Steele" or anyone who fit my great-grandfather's description in those records. I realized that regardless of where he was sent and what the school had taken from him, he returned to Mesita and his people because he wanted to serve them. He did so by becoming a federal civil servant with the Bureau of Indian Affairs. In addition to farming, he worked as a BIA policeman.

A generation later, the Catholic Church took both my grandparents from their families and communities as eight-year-old children. My grandmother told me that a priest came around to the houses to "gather the children and to put them on the train." I tried to imagine what that had been like. What would a priest tell a mother to convince her to give up her children? Or did they take the children without their parents' knowledge or consent? I know that in many communities across the country, priests and city folk were sent out to do the federal government's bidding, taking children against their parents' will. Some families hid their children when the authorities came around. The loneliness, physical and mental abuse, foreign surroundings, and foreign food would change a child forever. It created a great rift within families, between those who were forced to leave and those who stayed behind.

In many cases, boarding school survivors returned to their communities unable to speak their native languages. If they were lucky, they had opportunities to relearn and reacquire what they had lost—or, rather, what the federal government, the boarding schools, and the teachers had stolen from them—thereby defying the odds. My grandparents both spoke their native languages fluently, and after their marriage, my grandfather became a fluent Keres speaker out of respect for my grandmother.

My grandma talked about the boarding school—about the loneliness she endured and about how she and the other girls cleaned the church, peeled potatoes, sewed, and ironed. The boys, she said, farmed, built, and fixed things. It was clear from her stories that the schools were not meant to help Indigenous children succeed academically, but rather to train them as servants. The impacts of this education changed Native communities for generations, keeping Indigenous families in the lower tiers of society and inflicting deep and lasting pain. In some cases, after the children were taken away, their families never saw them again; there are school cemeteries to prove it.

The reverence with which the people of my pueblo view our mission churches was centuries in the making. During the assimilation era, many of our country's religious denominations inflicted cruelty in keeping with the federal policy to beat the culture, traditions, and Native languages out of Indigenous children. Regardless of the heartache the Church inflicted, many Laguna people are deeply religious. My grandmother prayed every bead on her rosary before bed, and responsibilities to the Church didn't end at home.

When I was in sixth grade at Laguna Elementary School, a big yellow school bus would drop us all off at church about once a week. Nuns, all in gray habits, would greet us, standing like a gauntlet with their arms outstretched to nab any kids who tried to run away before leading us into church for catechism. We learned how people become saints and the names of the patron saints of the Laguna Pueblo churches. They taught us about Jesus dying on the cross and why we receive Communion wafers during church services. I still remember Sister Mariam, who had a gentle smile and a calm, mellifluous voice. In contrast with another sister who once kicked our beloved dog Queenie out from under the pew with her pointed black shoes, Sister Mariam was kind to us and seemed to enjoy the Catholic lessons she taught.

We have elected or appointed officials in our tribal governments who are responsible for the upkeep of the Catholic churches in each of our villages. "Happy Feast Day" resonates in our villages on the saints' days the Franciscan priests designated centuries ago, and we observe those saints' days by dancing, singing, cooking, and opening our homes to visitors.

It was at St. Catherine's Catholic Indian School, located near the Veterans National Cemetery off Highway 84 in Santa Fe, that my grandparents met as children. When they attended in the early 1900s, the school may have been on the outskirts of town, with nary another building or house for miles. My grandmother told me that she came back to Mesita around 1921, when she was thirteen. She would wake at dawn to herd sheep for her father. She learned how to tend her dad's field and preserve the food they grew, and she cooked while indulging in the joys of pueblo life and spending time with her mother.

My grandfather went back to Jemez, where I suspect he returned to farming, hunting, and ceremonial obligations, although I never had the chance to speak with him about that time in his life.

In the mid-1920s, my grandmother went to Winslow,

Arizona, about three and a half hours west of Mesita Village. Her sister had moved there with her husband, and she asked my grandmother to come live with them and help care for their children. When my grandfather learned that my grandmother was relocating to Winslow, he went to Laguna Feast to see her.

In those days, men from the Atchison, Topeka, and Santa Fe Railroad, known as the AT&SF, often came to the pueblo to recruit workers as part of an agreement they'd made in the late 1800s, when the transcontinental railroad began laying track through New Mexico. They needed the Laguna Pueblo's permission to lay track through Indian land, and they negotiated the easement by promising jobs to any Laguna member who wanted one, women included. The company used feast days and other community gatherings to sign people up to work in various towns along the train route. Many Lagunas worked on the railroad in New Mexico, Arizona, and California, joining thousands of Pueblo people who were part of massive relocation programs that pushed them away from their homes to become plumbers, electricians, clerk typists, and other blue-collar workers. The general view at the time was that if Indians were taken off their lands and separated from their communities, they would essentially become white people. The politicians and others who held this view underestimated people like my grandparents.

On the spot, my grandfather signed up to work for the railroad in Winslow. He and my grandmother were married there and lived in a compound of old boxcars arranged in rows and surrounded by a fence adjacent to the railroad yard. The Pueblo people who worked at the railroad had only a short walk to their shifts, which was good, because many did not own cars.

According to my mother, the compound had community bathrooms and communal outdoor mud ovens; there was a plaza in the middle where people would dance for feast days, and the Laguna people built themselves a Laguna Pueblo village there. The Laguna Pueblo government referred to all the railroad boxcar communities as Laguna Colonies, but my mother always called the place where she grew up the Indian Camp.

She was born there in a boxcar in 1935, the youngest of four children. Old photos of their home show a wooden porch and a woodpile outside the door of the boxcar. My grandma made it nice for them by sewing curtains and keeping the place clean. My grandfather fixed anything that broke and kept the outside of the house in good order. When my mother was old enough to wield an ax, it became her job to chop wood so my grandmother could cook on the wood-burning stove.

My grandfather and other men from the Indian Camp must have worked hard and creatively to bring traditional ceremonies to the Laguna people in Winslow. I was about three years old when I watched my first dance at the Indian Camp. The people also celebrated Laguna Pueblo feast days, honoring the Catholic saints of our respective six villages. That in itself must have been a challenge, considering that the Indian Camp did not have a Catholic saint dedicated to it, or even a church. I don't know what it took to bring traditional feast days to Winslow, but their arrival ensured that the people of the Laguna Pueblo Indian Camp could continue their traditions.

Grandpa Toya was a stocky man with thick forearms. I

mostly saw him in work clothes, although he wore a suit when someone got married and a clean white shirt when my grandmother scheduled a photographer to come to the house every once in a while to take portraits. At other times, he wore cuffed khaki trousers and a denim or flannel button-down shirt with the sleeves rolled up. He had a zippered jacket or hooded sweatshirt and wore a fedora or a railroad cap atop his short, thick black hair.

Whenever we were in Winslow as kids, my mother would take me to the railroad yard to collect my grandfather after his shift. I clearly remember him coming toward us, crossing the web of train tracks with his jacket slung across his back. I would relieve him of his lunchbox and immediately open it to see what leftovers he had. Only when I was much older did I realize that he always saved me part of his lunch on purpose—a deep-red apple or a few saltine crackers. Grandpa had nicknames for all of us. He called my sister Zoe Norske because we were Norwegian and me Twister because, thanks to Elvis Presley, I incessantly danced the twist. Grandpa painted "TWISTER" in red paint on the back of my yellow chair.

Before her children were born, my grandmother also went to work for the railroad. Grandma cleaned diesel train engines, and she managed a night shift of women who scrubbed the engines clean with buckets of kerosene and a brush. I have an old black-and-white photo of my grandmother in her denim work overalls and blue collared shirt staring into the camera—a serious woman with a serious job navigating a colonized world.

Grandma would labor through the night ridding the diesel engines of the gunk and debris that accumulated over time and sending the trains out on time early in the morning, a great service to our country in the midst of industrialization. Then she would return to the family's boxcar home to make breakfast and get my mom and her siblings off to school. She eventually was able to quit the railroad job and work at home, and when I say "work," I mean it. My grandma worked from sunup to sundown. She took pride in the way she cleaned, cooked, and ran her household, and she had very high standards for how she cared for the houses we lived in and the people she loved.

Watching my grandmother clean and organize the house and us, I eventually came to realize that she had learned her obsessive housekeeping skills at boarding school. The nuns must have drilled cleanliness into the children, because Indians were thought to be dirty. My grandmother woke before sunrise every morning and cleaned her house from top to bottom. When we stayed with her, we were sent outside to play from morning until bedtime, and even my grandfather never sat on the furniture, to avoid getting it dirty; in Winslow, he watched TV lying on the floor with his head propped up on interlaced fingers. I remember this fondly because I would emulate him. My aunt told me that she once found my grandfather brushing his teeth outside because my grandma had already cleaned the bathroom, and he didn't want to mess it up.

Beyond the boarding schools, anti-Indian stigma persisted. My mother spoke candidly about being beaten on the hands with a section of green rubber garden hose whenever a Keres word came out of her mouth at the public school she attended in Winslow. My mother's kindergarten graduation photo shows most of her classmates smiling, but I see anger and sadness on her face.

She spoke once of a time at school when the Indian children were given sour milk instead of the fresh milk given to the white children. She didn't know whether it was intended to save the school money or to punish the Native kids. She went home and complained to her dad. My grandfather was a natural-born leader who always believed that he and the Pueblo people he lived and worked alongside deserved the same things white folks had. The next day, he stormed into the school, berating the leadership and reminding them that he, too, paid his taxes and that his children, like the others, deserved unspoiled milk.

Grandpa Toya was an athlete, an artist, and a musician. By the time my mother was in high school, he had taught her to play softball, keep score at a baseball game, read music, and play the snare drum. Long before Rosetta Stone and Google Translate, Grandpa could speak Towa, Keres, and English fluently, as well as some Spanish, Hopi, and Navajo. When I consider my grandfather's many talents and what he was capable of, I often think that he would have thrived at an educational institution worthy of his brilliant mind and spirit, but such institutions were closed to men like him. Instead, he became a diesel train mechanic. He would drive "the wrecker," a vehicle with all the tools and supplies needed to fix trains, out to the middle of the Arizona desert where stranded trains lay dead on the tracks, and wherever the trains were, he would work to get them moving again. Sometimes he stayed out for days at a time.

My grandparents built a life in Winslow, where they bought a three-bedroom home on Navajo Drive in the Desert View subdivision. The two guest rooms had a Jack-and-Jill closet, which was my favorite thing about the house. I'd go in and out of the closet, from one room to the next, until Grandma got annoyed and sent us outside to play. A chain-link fence surrounded the front yard, and a tall redwood picket fence surrounded the back, separating it from an alley that ran behind the house.

Grandpa always had many goals and worked to achieve them. When my grandmother needed a bedroom added to the house in Mesita, he built it. When my auntie Ann started a new position at the Indian Health Service hospital in Shiprock, he made a nameplate for her desk in the shape of Shiprock, that extraordinary New Mexico geologic formation that the Navajo people called "Winged Rock." And when he realized that the boys from the Indian Camp needed to play baseball, he started a team.

He involved the whole family in all his endeavors, but baseball was his favorite. My uncles played on the team, my cousin was a batboy, my mom kept score, and my grandma and auntie Ann ran the concession stand. Grandpa would pay my cousins and me a nickel for every foul ball we retrieved. He called the team the Winslow Redskins. Names like that are now viewed as racist, but it's almost as if he took the name away from our antagonists. The team won regional and state championships, and there were always tall trophies on the fireplace mantel at the house on Navajo Drive.

I loved being with my grandparents, and when my dad was sent for his first tour of duty in Okinawa, we moved in with them at the house on Navajo Drive along with our beagle puppy,

Queenie. One early morning, something terrible happened. My sisters and I were still in our pajamas and Queenie was in the front yard, inside the chain-link fence, when my mom saw a dog catcher stop his vehicle, get out, and shoot Queenie with a tranquilizer gun before speeding off down the street. Queenie, terrified, hopped the fence and fled. A great commotion ensued, and my mom ran down the street to find our beloved dog.

My sisters and I cried and hugged for what seemed like hours. When my mom returned without Queenie, we went out to the backyard. The back gate was open, and when we looked left down the alley, we saw my grandpa carrying Queenie, one of her eyes dangling from its socket. That image is seared into my mind as I write this. To me, it is what heroism looks like.

My mother rushed Queenie to the vet, but the dog catcher's tranquilizer gun cost her an eye. That day, Queenie became my grandfather's dog.

CHAPTER 3

Soul Food

It was on Navajo Drive that I learned to cook by watching my grandmother. When Grandma was in the kitchen, she worked fast and wasn't one to make room for kids, so I spied on her from my perch on the redwood picnic table under the back porch, cupping my eyes with my hands at the kitchen window. My grandmother, in cotton stockings secured just above her knees, cotton dress, cross-stitch apron, and permed jet-black hair, moved with grace and purpose from kitchen table to stove to sink. She cooked every single day, making either that day's meals or corn and other foods for the days to come. My grandfather generally grew both blue and white corn in his field at Mesita, and Grandma processed both kinds, boiling the dried corn with ashes, which separated the outer shell of each kernel from the germ. She would drain the cooked corn in a yucca basket in the backyard, steam rising like a plume, before turning the white corn into posole, or hominy, and the blue into tortillas. While I watched, she sometimes forcefully kicked open the screen door with the back of her right foot and exited with a pot of boiling white corn. Other times, she'd bring out trays and trays of round, yeast-risen loaves that jiggled delicately as she walked to the mud oven.

To make tortillas, Grandma would spread the freshly cooked blue kernels between white cotton tea towels on the kitchen table to cool. I would lift the towels when she wasn't looking and nibble several kernels of the warm, soft corn. The rich, earthy smell of corn will always bring back memories of my grandmother simmering, grinding, and then patting soft, warm ground corn into fresh, thick tortillas. To accompany them, she would make a big pot of ground beef and red chile. She would shred cheese and lettuce and chop tomatoes and onions. My mom would assemble our blue corn enchiladas like open-faced sandwiches with all the toppings. We always ate together as a family, and dinner was the best time of the day.

A bright line separates male and female roles in traditional Pueblo societies. My grandfather provided. He earned the paycheck, chopped the wood, hunted the deer, grew the food, and carried out his part of our customs and traditions. My grandmother ensured that they lived within their means. She processed the food Grandpa brought home, cleaned and polished the house and all its contents, and met his every need for nourishing food, loving companionship, and laundered and pressed clothing. Once, Grandma sent us a photo of my grandfather sitting at the kitchen table with a three-tiered, chocolate-frosted birthday cake with candles on the top. The caption on the back of the photo read, "I baked Dad a three-story cake for his birthday." Grandma's food went beyond sustenance; it fed our souls, too.

Grandpa built a mud oven for my grandmother in the

backyard in Winslow, and the first time she started a fire to bake bread, a neighbor called the fire department, and a fire truck came screaming down the street and parked in front of her house. After that, the local newspaper, the Winslow *Reminder*, printed a notice saying that if anyone saw smoke coming from the vicinity of Helen Toya's house, there was no cause for alarm; it was probably just a fire in her mud oven.

Sometimes Grandma would use the mud oven to roast corn my grandfather harvested from his field in Mesita. He would often take me down to his cornfield, where I helped him to irrigate, hoe weeds, and pick worms off the corn. I would rather have been with my older sisters and cousins, but they would sneak out of the house without telling me. I was the youngest girl, and I was often left behind.

The agricultural fields at Mesita are below and to the north of the village. We often walked there, hoes and rakes in hand, but if Grandpa had a harvest to bring up to the house, we'd ride the short half mile or so on the dirt road in his blue Chevy pickup. Many fields were laid out there in the mineral-rich soil, the product of long-ago volcanos. To the north of those fields is the Rio San José, and north of that, the railroad tracks, and then the mesa. Standing in the field with the red mesa looming over everything was humbling. Next to it, the trains seemed like tiny toys making their way to some unknown destination.

Once while we were in the field, my grandfather made me eat one of the green worms I'd picked off the corn. He told me I would never have stomach problems if I ate it. Out of respect, I did as he said, with no argument. I've never had stomach problems, but whether that's because I ate that worm as a child I'll never really know. I give the credit to my grandfather, even if he was playing a trick on me.

Corn is a foundational crop of the Pueblo Indians, and my ancestors were some of our country's first agriculturalists, planting the "three sisters," corn, beans, and squash, in the quiet valleys and subtle canyons of places like Gran Quivira, Chaco Canyon, and Pecos Pueblo in New Mexico and Bears Ears in Utah. When planted together, the three sisters are complementary, supplying and absorbing important minerals from the soil so that all three thrive. When eaten together, they provide the balance of protein and nutrients our bodies need to be healthy. Our songs, dances, images, and rituals have always sought to preserve the land and the Pueblo way of life for future generations, and that meant ensuring sustenance with every passing year.

Historically, various types of corn yielded different ingredients for stews and bread. When the Spanish came to the Southwest in the mid-1500s, they brought livestock, the conical outdoor *hornos* we call mud ovens, and wheat, which the Pueblo Indians quickly began using in their staple foods. Now our Pueblos are known for our oven bread. But our songs, traditions, and art involve corn. We pray with ground corn; corn has been and always will be a part of us.

Roasting whole sweet corn in a mud oven requires that the husks stay intact when a harvest of corn is placed on the red embers of a cedarwood fire. We'd work quickly to toss the corn all at once into the domed oven, and then Grandma would pour a bucket of water through the hole in the top. She had mud ready in the wheelbarrow, and she would place a flat rock on the top hole and seal the edges of the oven with mud before covering the opening at the front and sealing that with mud, too. We would then circle the oven and cake mud over any gaps where we saw steam emanating. This process usually took place in the evening; in the early morning, we would go outside, break the seal, and see our beautiful prize. Warm, roasted sweet corn is one of the best things in the world to eat. The flavor of the corn, harvested at the peak of its sweetness, intertwines with the smoky aroma of cedar and makes all the work worthwhile.

We'd pull the roasted corn from the still-warm oven and spread the ears to cool in large metal tubs. We would peel back the husks and use them to tie two ears of corn together so we could hang them to dry under the porch. After several days or a week, Grandma and I would rub two of the whole ears together over the big metal tub to dislodge the kernels. Grandma stored the kernels in cloth flour sacks and took a cup or two out when she cooked sweet corn stew. She and my mother often made a stew with the roasted sweet corn, beef cubes, and roasted and peeled green chile.

"Chili" is short for *chili con carne*, which originated near the Texas-Mexico border, but New Mexico is known for its red and green chile, pronounced the same way but spelled with an *e*. Chile plants, an important part of our Pueblo agricultural tradition, blossom and produce green fruits that are six to eight inches long and pointed. When the green peppers are left on the plant to ripen in the sun, the chile turn from green to yellow, orange, and finally red. Green chile is generally roasted and peeled, while red chile is dried and crushed, ground, or blended into a puree. The flavors are completely different, and a person may develop a taste for one or the other, hence New Mexico's state question: "Red or green?"

After the Spanish brought wheat, Pueblo farmers became adept at growing, harvesting, and grinding it, and my grandmother's ancestors baked wheat bread to perfection. When baking bread, Grandma would begin by building a fire in the mud oven. I loved the smell of cedar smoke as the oven heated. When the fire was reduced to embers, she'd remove them with a long wooden pole to which she had attached a rag with wire. She would dip the rag into a bucket of water and swirl it around the hearth to clean out the embers and ashes. Once the oven was clean, she'd test it with dry oatmeal. I never timed how long it took for the oatmeal to burn or knew what temperature Grandma found acceptable before she placed the risen dough carefully on the hearth, but through the years, I have done the oatmeal test on the hearth myself, and my bread hasn't burned or been undercooked.

My grandpa and uncles would go deer hunting during the season, and once, on a Sunday night in Winslow when I was about four years old, I stood at the window waiting for them to come home until my mom finally made me go to bed. I awoke early the next morning and searched every room for my grandpa, but I couldn't find him. Grandma was in the kitchen, dressed and ready for the day even though it was still dark, making coffee and breakfast. I asked for Grandpa, and she said he was out in the garage.

I opened the door slowly to find four deer lying on the garage floor on blankets. They were lined up facing the same direction, and Grandpa was sleeping on a cot by their heads. He sat up as soon as I turned on the light. Even as a child, I knew enough about my grandfather to know that he had slept near the deer out of respect. The hunters had gotten in late and had not performed a ceremony to welcome the deer to our home or to properly send their spirits off. Grandpa had an obligation to stay with the deer until then.

After breakfast, we brought the deer inside. My grandma and mother laid woven kilts and belts across the animals' torsos. They placed rings and bracelets on their antlers and laid turquoise beads across their necks and moccasins near their feet. We all prayed with cornmeal, sprinkling it near the animals' mouths and rubbing it onto their antlers.

My grandpa and uncles took the deer outside and skinned and quartered them. My grandma and mom cut off pieces of meat, meticulously thinning large segments of deer thigh and leg with sharp knives. They salted and hung the pieces to dry, along with the ribs, on cotton rope they'd strung taut between the beams of the back porch.

An abundance of sun and a dry climate gave the Pueblo Indians a perfect way to preserve food: through dehydration. Drying meat, corn, and other foods is how my ancestors stored nourishment for the winter. I learned much later that when the Spanish settlers arrived, the people of Pecos Pueblo in Northern New Mexico, where my grandfather's family originated, had five years' worth of food stores for a population of two thousand people. My grandparents' industriousness has stayed with me since I was that child peering through the kitchen window in Winslow.

Drying deer meat is a time-intensive endeavor; fresh meat

is heavy, and there is so much of it. My grandma would hang the meat in the mornings and take it down before it got dark outside. A week or so later, once the meat had dried, we'd take it down for good. Some was stored for future meals, while some of the jerky and ribs were made into deer stew. "You must make the stew with things that deer like to eat," my grandma told me, like dried sweet corn, hominy, and the local pine nuts known as piñons.

When a member of the community brings home a deer, it is customary to host a deer supper to share the abundance. Women prepare large pots of deer stew and bake bread, and family members drive around the village honking their horns and yelling out their car windows, "Deer supper!" We would take along cupcakes or a can of peaches for the host, and the men would be on hand to tell tales of the hunt. Antlers usually protruded from the steaming pot as the skinned head cooked. Deer head was a prized delicacy reserved for the hunters' aunties.

For eons, our sustenance depended on the food my ancestors grew, hunted, and preserved. Stew is still our traditional food, but the methods of cooking and obtaining ingredients have changed. When the Spanish brought seven thousand head of livestock to the Southwest in the early 1500s, beef became a stand-in for deer. Today, we don't always grow our own corn, beans, and squash or even hunt, but the food my grandma taught me to cook will always be considered traditional in Laguna, regardless of whether I grow the ingredients or purchase them at the store.

My grandmother was dedicated to ensuring that our traditions continued, so she cooked stew and baked bread for all our ceremonies. She shared with me the intricacies of her deer stew and the prayers she recited while it cooked. I learned from her both a profound respect for the animals who give their lives so that we can live and the practice of giving something in return for the earth's daily gifts.

One clear, warm morning when I was eleven, Grandma took me to visit her brother Grandpa Manuel, who lived under the blue blanket of sky with six dogs and dozens of sheep. Perhaps he hadn't chosen to become a shepherd, but he lived up to an inheritance that was hard to shun. Growing up, Manuel and my grandmother had cared for sheep and knew them as family. Perhaps it was the way the soft lambs looked at birth and how much they needed the guidance of a skillful and compassionate human being.

Manuel might have been lonely and frightened as a visitor in the animals' domain, but he chose to live away from the village from an early age and knew nothing else. Tsiyuiyea (si-u-E-ye) was his Indian name, and he herded sheep almost all his life. His secluded and demanding existence allowed him to come in only for supplies, feast days, and the sacred ceremonies held twice a year, and he enjoyed a place of high honor where aspects of our Indian culture were concerned. I heard a story that once, he came into the village complaining of a sore leg. He lifted his trousers to reveal a leg swollen with pus from a snakebite. He could survive anything: harsh winters, brutal summers, the pangs of raw nature.

His house stood between two small mesas and a vast expanse of flat, high desert dotted with cedar trees, grama grass, and basalt flows. We called it the Sheep Camp. Back then, Grandma drove a big blue GMC truck with a white top that she used to get places fast and to brush up on her swearing. In this case, I knew I would be safe, because the road to Grandpa Manuel's was dirt and deserted.

Grandma covered her head with a red plaid woolen scarf and secured it with a knot under her chin. Her purple-and-white checkered dress swayed above cotton stockings. We loaded the back of the pickup with bags of canned goods, beans, and other supplies and headed west. The windows were open, and my long, dark hair was a flag in the wind.

Twenty minutes later, we arrived at Grandpa Manuel's tiny basalt rock house surrounded by sheep corrals. Grandma had warned me not to open the truck door until Grandpa Manuel had called off his dogs, so we waited in silence while they barked uncontrollably. Though not particularly large, they were highly trained and vicious. Grandpa Manuel had taught them to protect the sheep at any cost.

Grandpa Manuel came out of his house in Levi's and a red flannel shirt. His skin was dark and wrinkled, and I could see his short black hair under his wide-brimmed felt cowboy hat. He walked with a slight limp. "*Sro-he'me*," he shouted: "That's enough." I assumed his dogs understood no English. They retreated from the truck, and we got out.

We entered the house through a thick pine door, carrying armloads of groceries in brown paper bags. A large, oval laundry basket held the bread my grandma had baked the day before. The mud floor smelled of sweet earth as we walked toward the kitchen table. Across the room was a single iron bed with a feather mattress, an army blanket, and a kerosene lamp atop a dingy nightstand. A small mirror, two oak chairs, a wood-burning stove, and two wash basins—one for his personal grooming, the other for his dishes—were all Grandpa Manuel's remaining furniture. He had no electricity and no running water. Someone from the village always hauled water for him in large metal barrels, which he kept outside the front door. He cooked his own meals, washed his clothes on a washboard, and made his own shoes, using old tires as soles.

After unloading the groceries, we stepped from the cool darkness of the rock house into the brilliant sunshine. We followed Manuel to the first corral, where he carefully chose the right sheep, led it to the north side of the house, roped it by its hind legs, and hoisted it up with a pulley attached to a wooden frame.

Once he secured the sheep, he carefully cut the length of its underside, opened the belly, and coaxed out the entrails. He pulled the intestines away from the other warm insides and squeezed from one end to the other, expelling their contents into a pile on the ground. Manuel asked my grandmother which parts she wanted, and she set a pan on the ground for the intestines, stomach, lungs, and liver.

Crouching quietly next to Grandma, I watched as he let the sheep down and, starting with the front legs, skinned and quartered everything but the head. He placed the meat gently into the pickup. This was all done very quickly and with great fondness. I found myself appreciating the methodical actions of this old man so familiar with sheep.

Soon, Grandma and I were whizzing down the road again under the high sun. When we got home, Grandma wasted no time putting the sheep's head into a pan and then into a warm oven. She tended to the remaining mutton, cutting it into logical pieces. She hung the ribs on a bent coat hanger and affixed the coat hanger to a nail on the front porch frame.

Several hours later, when the sheep's head had reached the perfect temperature, Grandma pulled it from the oven. Usually, mealtimes were consistent, and we all ate together, but this was a special occasion. Grandma laid a kitchen towel on the tablecloth and placed the baking pan with the sheep's head on top of it. She used a sharp knife to carefully peel back and then discard the baked brown fur before gratefully savoring her delicacy with green chile and bread.

CHAPTER 4

My Norwegian Side

My great-grandfather Thor Håland was from Kvitsøy Island, off the southwestern coast of Norway in the North Sea. He lived there in a house with a pitched slate roof and a white picket fence on a farm that bore his family's name. Great-grandfather Håland was a farmer and, of course, a fisher. He would row his boat from Kvitsøy to Skudeneshavn to court my great-grandmother. During World War II, the German army took over Kvitsøy and used his house as officers' quarters.

By that time, the Håland family was long gone. They had sent my great-grandfather's youngest brother, Peder, to the United States first. Peder sent back photos and letters about his life in Iowa, where he told his brothers he'd made friends with the Indians. From the black-and-white photos I saw years later, I couldn't determine what tribes he'd engaged with, but there was Peder, in trousers, a work shirt, and suspenders, standing in a village with conical mud huts in the background.

Eventually, my great-grandparents followed Peder to Iowa, where they spent several years before putting down roots in Minnesota. I never met my paternal grandfather, Conrad Haaland, but he honored his parents' agrarian tradition, and my father had many fond memories of his childhood on the farm. In one photo, my dad is wearing a pair of overalls and a collared shirt and holding a rope attached to a fish that is longer than his body. In another, his sister Mary is holding a bucket and feeding a cow.

My grandfather's first wife and my dad's mother, Gunhild Johanna Jacobsen Haaland, died of cancer when my father was a young teen. Throughout my childhood, we spent time with Grandpa's second wife, Mae, when she came to visit or when we visited her, which was not often. We called her Grandma Haaland to distinguish her from Grandma Helen.

Grandma Haaland had been raised in Chicago and worked for the Daly City Colma Chamber of Commerce. After my grandfather passed away, she returned to Chicago before moving into a senior community in Florida, where the over-chlorinated pool made our eyes burn. Grandma Haaland had tight white curls and cat-eye glasses, and with her lipstick, neatly pressed blouses, and jewelry, she always looked ready to be somewhere. Even though my father was older when she came into his life, I sensed that he had the deepest respect for her, so I went out of my way to show her affection when we visited.

My aunt Anne—my namesake, and not to be confused with my maternal auntie Ann—was my dad's older sister. She was thin like my dad, and she had beautiful red hair. We often stopped to visit her and my cousins in San Mateo, California, on our way from one place to another, sometimes staying three or four nights. She was a cashier at the neighborhood grocery, and when she went off to work in the morning, my mother managed me and my sisters for a deep clean of Aunt Anne and Uncle Bob's house. That was how we spent many family vacations at various relatives' houses. My mother had an idea of what "clean" meant, and she endeavored to spread that idea wherever we went.

Aunt Anne and Uncle Bob had a large wooden dining room table with at least a dozen chairs. After the evening meal was done and the kids had washed the dishes, we'd bring out the cards, and our two families would play spoons and other games for many hours. Once, my cousin Carol, who could drive before any of the rest of us, took us to the ice-skating rink. It was my first time on ice skates, and my ankles were sore afterward.

My aunt Anne once told me that when the US government began giving subsidies to Minnesota farmers in the mid-1940s, my Grandpa Conrad refused to "take a handout." Instead, he sold his farm and moved to San Francisco, where he answered an ad in a local newspaper for shipbuilders. World War II was raging, and everyone was expected to serve. I greatly admire my grandfather's courage in changing careers at that point in his life. Three of his four children were grown, and he could have chosen an easy retirement, but our country needed him.

My dad, John David Haaland, was in his early teens when Grandpa Conrad moved the family to the Hunters Point neighborhood of San Francisco. He joined the JROTC in high school, and at eighteen, he decided to join the US Marines. My dad once told me that while sitting at a bus stop one day in downtown San Francisco, he was approached by a man dressed in a suit and carrying a briefcase who asked him if he wanted to be in a Marlboro cigarette ad. I can imagine my dad, in a starched shirt, tailored trousers, and a stylish haircut, smiling widely and smoking, the perfect young man to sell cigarettes to men of the Silent Generation who were coming of age with Chuck Berry and Frank Sinatra. It might have been the start of a different career, but my dad said no. He told the man with the briefcase that he was joining the marines the next day.

His photo as a new recruit—in a crisp green summer uniform, tie, and stiff-billed cap known as a cover—radiates joy and sincere pride. The United States had emerged triumphant from World War II by then, defeating the evils of mass genocide and Nazism, and patriotic fervor was running high. In all the years I knew him, my father remained proud and optimistic about his service and our country, and he passed those feelings on to me and my siblings.

The military brought my parents together. My mom joined the navy as a young woman, and she and my father were both assigned to the now-defunct Naval Station Treasure Island, in San Francisco Bay. A mutual friend and member of the Cherokee Nation, Gene Brandon, introduced them. My mother often talked about having seen Elvis Presley perform live in San Francisco on one of her first dates with my dad. Before the show, my father treated her to $1.99 all-you-can-eat spaghetti at a local diner. While my mom reveled in the King's stage presence and concertgoers danced in the aisles, she recalled that Dad kept going outside to smoke cigarettes.

Dutch was the nickname my dad's troops gave him, a play on his surname, which was pronounced like *Holland*, but his family called him by his middle name, Dave. Dave "Dutch" Haaland would go on to serve nearly thirty years in the US

Marines, including two tours in Vietnam. He became what military people call a mustang, a commissioned officer who starts his military career at an enlisted rank. He earned his commission not by going to college, but because of his aptitude for leadership. While in Vietnam for twenty-six consecutive months, he was promoted to second lieutenant. After the war, many officers were demoted to save the country money, but at his next duty station, in Virginia Beach, my dad spent hours upstairs in the bedroom I shared with my sister in our house on Kenneth Road studying to hold on to what he had accomplished. He had earned his commission through great sacrifice, and he kept passing tests to retain his rank. He was promoted to captain and then major. Attaining the higher ranks was a testament to his dedication, courage, and confidence, but also to my mother's hard work and discipline. She washed and ironed all his uniforms throughout his career, and although she had served in the navy, because of my dad, she was a marine at heart. His sacrifices were also hers.

In Vietnam, my dad was awarded a Silver Star "for conspicuous gallantry" in saving the lives of six other marines. He spoke to me only once about his time there, when I interviewed him for a college essay I was writing. I asked if he ever felt that the war in Vietnam had been prolonged because of politics, or that the United States should never have been there in the first place. "Never," he told me. He said that he had signed up for the job, that was where the president had asked him to go, and it was his job to follow orders. He said that his number one objective was to keep as many of his troops alive as possible, and that was what he did. He thought about nothing else.

I knew Dutch Haaland was important by the large number of medals he wore on his chest whenever he put on his dress whites or blues, including two Purple Hearts. The medals were one manifestation of his sacrifices in service to our country. My mother told me that once, when we'd gone to pick him up at the airport after one of his many deployments, I was afraid of him and scurried to the back of the station wagon to get as far away from him as possible. He had been gone for many months, which seemed like years to me.

PART II
MOVING

FOR WATER

A fight for water, for land, begins at home. At the kitchen table, in the bath before bed, while your mother recites a story from her childhood. Our family traditions—to watch out for land, water, animals—to pray to and for them so that they will always be there. "Don't waste" was my mother's mantra. A mantra for the ages is to be careful with the things that keep us alive. Not one drop of water has come into or left our planet in 4.6 billion years. We have to make it last.

When I was a tender age, my grandma woke me at sunrise to fetch water. The sun casts a golden light on the red mesa at 6 a.m., and the dirt road is welcoming. A shallow pan was all anyone needed to begin a day. "*Paa-tch-a,*" "Let it rain," is what desert Indians say.

I'm here because my ancestors knew how to survive.

How to plant.

How to harvest.

How to collect water, dance, and pray for rain.

I'm here because my ancestors believed that living another day was worth my life. Giving is like receiving, and above all else, staying on the land our Mother beckoned us to, so many centuries ago, was her plan, not ours; the obligation works both ways.

It can now be determined that Indians should not perish from the earth but be fruitful and multiply. Annihilation was never meant to be. But the Indian wars are not yet finished, and the Indians are still fighting, still defending what is theirs—like their ancestors, defending the same water and the same land, a repeat of the not-so-ancient past.

"Indians have given enough," a wise Pueblo woman once said.

The Lakotas and the Dakotas and the White Earth people once lived on thousands of miles—like the buffalo, unencumbered, until fences and people and gunshot and cannons took their toll. The water is what they still have. What we all still have.

CHAPTER 5

Semper Fi

Growing up, we moved every few years. Once, we moved after only six months because that was what the Marine Corps asked of us. Everything we had, my parents would say, was thanks to "the Corps." By the time I graduated from high school, I had attended thirteen public schools, in California, Arizona, Virginia, and New Mexico. Even though moving was tedious and time-consuming, I did as I was told.

When I was a baby, we lived with my grandparents in Winslow before a stint in Oceanside, California, where my dad was stationed at Camp Pendleton. But my earliest memories are from our house on North C Street in Tustin, California, where my brother, John David Haaland Jr., was born when I was four years old. I had a friend there named Corinne who lived with her dad a couple of houses away; between us lived a mean old lady who always dressed in black. She had one of those big metal rods people used to turn on their sprinklers, and whenever we walked by her house with our dog on a leash, she would hit Queenie with it. We were terrified of her.

My dad liked dogs, and we had many growing up, but my

mom didn't care too much for them. As with so much else, she tolerated them for my dad's sake. Although Grandma and Grandpa Toya had never served in the armed forces, my mom belonged to a military family. Her two older brothers, Wilfred and Ben, both served in the navy, and Auntie Ann's husband, my uncle Paul, had served in the army. My mother's own short navy career ended when she became pregnant with my sister Denise. The policy that deemed pregnancy incompatible with military service would not change until 1975.

Whether because of her upbringing or her time in the military, my mom was predisposed to being disciplined and to disciplining. That was especially true when my dad was away and she was alone and anxious, a de facto single mother of four and prone to impatience with me and my siblings. In Tustin, I had a stuffed owl that I loved. It had orange wings, an orange beak, and big owl eyes. My mother knew how much I liked it, and one day, she ripped one of its wings off. That made me terribly sad. "I've had it up to here with you!" she would say when she got angry, placing her hand to her forehead like a salute. Sometimes it was difficult to predict what we should be doing from one day to the next, but I quickly learned to do most of what my mom required: to make my bed, pick up my things, and do my schoolwork.

Through family stories, I learned that my mom's relationship with her own mother had been troubled. Her parents had sent her to St. Catherine's, the same oppressive boarding school they had attended—and they did so by choice, not because anyone forced them. I regret that I didn't talk more with my mother about her childhood, but she seemed scarred by it. For some reason, I felt that she was especially hard on me. Through her, I inherited the curse of the Indian Boarding Schools.

My mother demanded much from others, but even more from herself. When I was growing up, she liked to say that our home was well kept. In reality, my siblings and I were spit and polished, and the military shone through in every floor tile and every bed my dad could bounce a quarter on. As kids, we never argued with our parents. We learned discipline. The thick skin I grew has served me well. A career public servant is bound to get yelled at. That never bothered me much because I was used to it.

I started kindergarten at four, and I was always the youngest pupil in my class, which I found embarrassing. When a teacher would ask how old we were, I would shrink into myself. In first grade, I didn't want to raise my hand for anything because I was only five while everyone else was six.

I was also often the only Native American in my classroom, and at each new school, I was charged with making new friends. My mother cared about appearances. She would tightly braid my sisters' and my hair and send us out starched and pressed, as if she knew we would be judged more harshly than others. Most of my wardrobe consisted of my sisters' hand-me-downs, and my sisters got their clothes from one of our older cousins, but they were spotless.

I didn't realize that other students saw me as different or inferior until one day, when I was five or six, one of my classmates stopped me on the sidewalk and told me that I had a "fat face, fat ears, fat legs, and fat braids." I think she even poked me on the shoulder. I looked at her somewhat puzzled and kept walking home. I never told my mother what had happened. For the first time, I felt shame about the way I looked.

I didn't understand the politics of diversity, or the lack thereof, as a kid. But my dad did. In 1948, President Truman had issued an executive order to desegregate the armed forces, including the Marine Corps, so my dad was very cognizant of the value of diversity among the troops he led. We learned from him.

We moved to San Clemente in 1965. I remember the day we went looking for a house there. It was pouring, and my father drove us around town to see different properties. "What house do you girls like best?" he asked. We saw a two-story house with a second-floor balcony. It was raining so hard that we mistook the balcony for a swimming pool. We all chose that one.

The house didn't have a pool, but it was beautiful. Property must have been cheap back then for my dad to have been able to afford the rent.

During the holiday season, I loved to watch my dad prepare an overabundance of traditional Norwegian Fattigmann cookies, and we practiced many of his family traditions, including eating hot rice with cream, sugar, and cinnamon on Christmas Eve. He would place a pinto bean in the pot of rice, and whoever ended up with the bean in their bowl would have the honor of passing out the gifts from under the tree.

I remember a Christmas morning in San Clemente, still in pajamas with my sisters. After finding the Christmas stockings Santa had hidden the night before, we happily inspected their contents. My mom didn't have fancy Christmas stockings, so she used my dad's Marine Corps–issue socks, which she filled with fruit and nuts instead of candy. It was a special occasion, so my mother had put our hair in sponge curlers before bed. My brother's hair was easy back then. He always had a buzz-cut flattop, courtesy of my mom's own clippers.

We moved to San Diego next, where my dad was a drill instructor at the Marine Corps Recruit Depot, known as MCRD. He lived on base with his troops during the week and came home on weekends to our turquoise house with white trim on Jemez Drive. People there pronounced the street name as "JIM-ez," and my mom would roll her eyes, but she never corrected them. We all knew it was pronounced "HAY-mish," like the name of my grandfather's pueblo.

While in San Diego, we looked forward to driving to MCRD to watch the military parades, where my dad's troops would perform expert rifle-assembly drills and march in formation. Each parade began with the Pledge of Allegiance and "The Star-Spangled Banner," and we stood at attention. My dad always seemed proud of how his troops performed, both on the field and in the bleachers. He cared deeply for them. During one of our visits to Washington, DC, my dad took us to see the Sunset Parade at the Marine Corps Barracks on Eighth and I Streets. It was a memorable evening, with the Drum and Bugle Corps and the Marine Corps Band playing, along with the silent drill team. Watching the marines perform precision drill sequences made me proud of the work my father did, although it never quite inspired me to join the marines myself.

My brother is my youngest sibling, and we called him J.D. for short. One of my dad's troops, who eventually became a good friend and whom we knew as Uncle Les, couldn't pronounce "J.D.," so the two syllables eventually morphed into "Judd," and the name stuck. When my brother was a kid, he had a distinct enthusiasm for water, and he would grab the hose in the front yard without warning, turn on the water, and just start spraying. He would crouch in a strategic position as if he were defending Fort Haaland, his tiny Chuck Taylors sinking into mud puddles, a devious little smirk on his face. If you happened to be walking down the sidewalk, you'd get soaked. We treated it like a fire drill—"J.D. has the hose!" One of us would sound the alarm, and my mother would dash around the house closing the windows before running out to turn off the spigot.

One of the best things about being a military kid was living near other military kids. Whether we lived in base housing or in neighborhoods close to bases, there were many families with children, and we played nearly every day for hours. We once lived near a family that was Native Hawaiian. When it was time for the kids to go home, their mom would stand outside and blow through a large conch shell, making a loud, hornlike sound that could be heard for blocks. No matter what we were doing, as soon as our Hawaiian playmates heard that sound, they'd drop everything and run home. My mom had a knack for whistling through two fingers, which was how we knew it was time for dinner. At one of my dad's duty stations, we lived in a house connected to a long row of other houses by a single front lawn that stretched the length of the block. There were no fences between the properties, and we could run and play forever.

Being raised in a military family and learning to follow orders as a child prepared me for the life of a Pueblo woman. My siblings and I started spending summers in Winslow and Mesita when I was five or six years old. When my dad was stationed in San Diego, my grandma came out from Winslow, picked up Denise and me, and brought us back to Arizona on the train. She had a lifetime rail pass because of my grandfather's work on the railroad. I remember having to step between the cars while the train was moving. My grandfather was waiting for us when we arrived the next morning. At their house, my grandmother gave us new dresses and scheduled a photographer to come take our pictures.

My great-grandfather had hauled basalt rocks from a nearby quarry to build my grandma's quaint rectangular house in Mesita one rock at a time. In anticipation of his retirement, my grandpa would drive the three-plus hours from Winslow to Mesita on the weekends and work on the house, plastering the inside and outside, building the roof and wood floors, and installing the front door, three windows, and a wood-burning stove. Eventually, Grandpa built an interior wall to separate the kitchen and a bathroom from the front room, which had a taupe chenille couch and several beds we all shared when we visited.

Living without running water or electricity was great during the summer, when it stayed light until 9 p.m., but in winter, Grandma wasn't about to waste oil or candles on kids goofing around, and we'd go to bed as soon as it got dark. Even after my grandmother had grown used to the modern conveniences of her home in Winslow, she was profoundly adept with a woodstove and a wash pan. We all were. My mother gave us baths in a galvanized tub, and when we were old enough, my sister and I would grab the handles of the tub and haul out the dirty water ourselves. It was there that I learned the value of conservation. A shallow pan of water was all we needed to wash up in the morning, and no one ever wasted a drop.

Before he shipped out to Vietnam, my dad moved us to Yuma, Arizona, where my mom's brother Wilfred lived and worked as a high school physical education teacher. The Marine Corps Air Station in Yuma was where we went to the doctor if we were sick and where my mom shopped for groceries at the commissary. Once, while riding with my cousin on the back of a bicycle, my ankle got caught in the spokes. My mother took me to the MCAS dispensary, where a corpsman carried me from the car to the exam room, X-rayed me, and wrapped my foot and ankle in an ACE bandage.

Yuma was so hot during the summers that radio deejays would joke between "California Dreamin'" and "Paperback Writer" that you could fry an egg on the sidewalk. My mom would send us out to play in the mornings, and at lunchtime, she'd call us in and close all the drapes to keep the house cool. To amuse ourselves, we would dress our brother up in our clothes, play music, and dance.

In Yuma, my mom would scrub and wax our tile floors on her hands and knees. Then she'd put white cotton socks on us so we could slide around on the floor to buff the tiles to a bright shine. Our floors were so shiny and slick that when visitors walked in our front door, they would often slip on the rugs, both feet flying into the air before they landed. My mother would apologize profusely every time, but her high standard of cleanliness never changed. I now understand that this was part of the painful boarding school experience she inherited from my grandmother, the anxious obsession with cleaning that was never satisfied, even when the floors were a fall risk.

My mother could be very strict. Maybe she sensed my rebellious nature even back then, long before it broke into the open. But she could be kind, too. She cared a great deal about the food she prepared and whether we enjoyed our meals. Macaroni and tomato soup was a favorite comfort food for us all. When my mother made us rolled enchiladas, I didn't like onions and Zoe didn't like cheese, so she would leave out the onions from mine and the cheese from Zoe's and mark our enchiladas with toothpicks among the dozens in the large pans. I always appreciated this, and I've found myself emulating it whenever I cook for children.

GREEN CHILE CHICKEN ENCHILADAS

1 whole chicken
3–4 cups chicken stock or water with soup base, as per instructions
2 dozen yellow corn tortillas
Vegetable oil for frying
½ yellow onion, diced
1 celery stalk, diced
1 garlic clove, minced
3 tbsp flour
Vegetable shortening to grease casserole dish

1 cup roasted, peeled, and chopped green chile
1 pound shredded medium cheddar or longhorn/ Monterey Jack cheese

Cook the chicken in a pot of water. (For best results, do this the day before.) Debone it and use the bones to make the chicken stock, if desired. Otherwise use a good chicken soup base or stock for flavor. Dice the meat.

To assemble the enchiladas: Fry the corn tortillas until crisp, standing them on end in a pan until all are fried.

Heat a few tablespoons of oil in a 6-quart pot over medium heat. Add the onion, celery, and garlic and sauté, stirring occasionally until soft, about 10 minutes. Add the flour and stir until light brown in color. Turn off the heat and let cool for about 10 minutes. Add the stock or water and stir until smooth, then heat thoroughly, continuing to stir so no lumps form. Cook for several more minutes until the sauce thickens. Add the diced chicken and chopped green chile and turn up the heat. When thoroughly heated, turn off flame.

Grease and flour a 12- or 13-inch casserole dish and ladle a small amount of chicken and sauce onto the bottom. Lay the fried tortillas over the chicken and sauce and top with cheese. Continue to alternate layers of chicken and sauce, tortillas, and cheese, ending with cheese on top. If you don't use all the corn tortillas, you can eat the leftovers with salsa!

Bake at 350°F for about 45 minutes or until bubbly.

The older I got, the more I appreciated my mother's strength. Her pain was often ours, and in that era, the country cared little for the families of combat soldiers. The Vietnam War was unpopular, and people often blamed those who served. My mom was constantly sick with worry over whether my dad would live another day. She would sometimes light a candle in the middle of the kitchen floor, and we would all kneel and say the rosary for my dad. She also often sat us down at the kitchen table to write him letters. She wrote to him nearly every day and sent care packages with food from home, writing paper, pens, and powdered drink mixes. She would draw *Peanuts* cartoons on the backs of her letters and make up captions for them. One day, some marines came to our house. After speaking with them for a few short minutes, my mother slumped in tears against the living room wall. We later learned that my dad had been wounded.

My mother never forgot those experiences or my dad's service. Many years later, when I was a teenager and we were living in Albuquerque, I got sick. The timing was inconvenient because my mother was busy cooking that day, likely for a ceremony at Laguna. She took me to Kirtland Air Force Base, just a few blocks from our house on Indiana Street SE, dropped me off outside the dispensary, and told me to call her when I was finished. By that time, I had my own military ID card and could manage some things on my own, although I did not drive.

To my great dismay, the medical staff said they would not see me because my dad was no longer on active duty. I called for a ride home, but when my mother arrived, she stormed through the doors and explained in the most forceful terms that my father was a decorated Marine Corps officer who had been in

Vietnam for two solid years and had served our country long before they could walk. She told them that they would see me immediately because my father had earned it. The corpsman said something like "Yes, ma'am" and took me right into the exam room.

CHAPTER 6

An All-American Childhood

After my dad returned from Vietnam, we packed up our house in Yuma and moved to Virginia Beach. My mother had won a small black-and-white television set in a drawing at a local appliance store in Yuma, and she put it in the kitchen so she and my dad could watch the evening news during dinner. It was fraught with images and stories of the fighting in Vietnam, and my dad would pound his fist on the table, sob, and say, "They're just kids."

My dad was stationed on the Little Creek naval base, and we lived in a mustard-yellow two-story house on Kenneth Road, where my three siblings and I shared two upstairs bedrooms. One day when I was in second or third grade, my older sisters said they planned to tell our parents they were sick, to get out of going to school. "We should all say we're sick and stay home," they urged. I refused. I was a straight-A student and very well behaved, and my teachers loved me. I hated the thought of a feigned sick day on my conscience, and besides, I knew that Smokey the Bear would be visiting our school that day. Normally, we all walked to school together, but that morning I got ready as usual and set off by myself. As I left the house, I looked up to see my sisters tapping on an upstairs windowpane, tears streaming down their faces. I guess I felt a little sad, too, but my desire to go to school outweighed my discomfort. When I returned that afternoon, my Smokey the Bear button pinned to my shirt, my sisters were laughing and pulling each other down the stairs on their bedroom pillows. I assessed that they hadn't spent too much time missing me.

Because of my secondhand childhood wardrobe, I still buy many of my clothes at thrift stores. Maybe that's why I so vividly remember the times my mother took us clothes shopping. One winter in Virginia Beach, she took my sister Zoe to Sears to pick out an outfit. Later, she took me there and suggested I try on the same thing my sister had chosen. Not knowing any better, I did as I was told. When we opened our presents on Christmas morning, Zoe and I looked at each other. We were old enough to find matching outfits embarrassing and to feel as if we had been played. If I had been a different kid, I might have refused to wear the outfit, but brand-new clothes were hard to come by, so I said nothing. Zoe and I made sure we didn't wear the outfit on the same day.

Alcohol was a fact of life in our household, and memories of grown-ups drinking are woven into my childhood. In Virginia, my parents would invite their friends over to play cards, smoke cigarettes, and drink beer late into the night. We kids would eventually put ourselves to bed. Lying there in the dark, I'd listen to the records playing on the turntable, memorizing the words to songs by Charley Pride, Merle Haggard, Johnny Cash, and Buck Owens.

My dad's childhood on a farm had given him a love of the outdoors that he passed on to us, and no matter where we lived, he wanted us to be outside. I have a black-and-white photo of my siblings, my dad, and me in the front yard of our house on Kenneth Road on the day of a solar eclipse. We made eclipse viewers and waited outdoors for the joyful moment when darkness would envelop us at midday.

I've realized as an adult that my dad's lessons were not always immediate or spoken aloud. He taught me to appreciate nature by being in it. His duty stations were often near the water, as the marines are the US military's amphibious force, and after breakfast on Sundays, he'd often say, "Let's go for a ride." I spent many days at the Pacific Ocean in San Diego and Oceanside and at the Atlantic Ocean and Chesapeake Bay in Virginia Beach and Norfolk; sometimes, my dad would make unplanned stops at beaches just to walk the shoreline. It was a wondrous experience to walk barefoot through the shallow water for what seemed like miles, with only the sound of ocean waves.

One of my dad's favorite places was the Jemez Mountains in New Mexico. We'd pack a picnic lunch and find a good place to park along the river. Once, we parked by Battleship Rock, and my siblings and I quickly unpacked the car and ran upward until we found our way to the precipice that defines this majestic pumice rock formation. My mom and dad looked tiny far below, and we called to them as loudly as we could, waving our arms and jumping up and down. We thought they would be proud of us, but my mother started yelling at us to come back down "right this instant!" As usual, we did not seem to grasp the danger associated with climbing upward, but my mother did. We quickly descended and waded through the cold river instead.

It could have been that trip or another when it started sprinkling, then raining, then pouring. My dad sat out there for a long time as if it were sunny and warm. We were soaked when he finally signaled that it was time to go home.

Every experience I've had in the outdoors has influenced how I see the world and has nurtured my respect for nature. There is no substitute for the real-time sound of a thousand geese taking flight from a body of still, black water, seeing a grandfather desert tortoise move with grace in a steep canyon overgrown with sagebrush and juniper, or a desert rain so hard you could swear the sky opened up.

During my elementary school years, our vacations didn't always seem like vacations. I sometimes learned that my classmates' parents were taking them to Disneyland, whereas my dad's idea of a good time was rowing a small boat on the Great Dismal Swamp. Once, in Virginia, my dad rented a rowboat, and we took in the sights by rowing for a few days. My sister Denise caught an eel and put it back into the water. Whenever our fishhooks snagged a tree branch, my dad would exclaim that we had "caught a tree fish!" I found the Dismal Swamp sadly lacking as a vacation spot, but I still remember a tree-lined passage with water like glass that perfectly reflected the trees. Over time, I gained a deep appreciation for that childhood vacation.

My dad recognized that we had a place in history, and he made sure we were aware of key events during our childhood. Because of him, I remember not just my first solar eclipse but also the day the first man walked on the moon, which we watched live on television. We were also among the 73 million people who watched the Beatles' premiere appearance on *The Ed Sullivan Show*, and my dad rousted us from bed to come downstairs to watch Elvis Presley's televised "Comeback" concert. I was only eight years old, but I still remember Elvis, dressed in his black leather jacket, alone on a small stage in the middle of an audience with his guitar.

When we lived in Virginia, it wasn't unusual for my mother to take us to the beach on the Little Creek naval base, and I now think she preferred that beach because it had marine lifeguards; she must have trusted them. Their presence allowed my mom to sink into the sand and read whatever book she was inhaling at the time. I can still see my sister Zoe and me in our one-piece swimsuits—hers bright yellow and mine red and white. That was the only swimsuit I had for as long as I could remember.

One day at the beach, while my mom got comfortable reading her book, we rode the waves on our rafts. We must have thought paddling out farther would give us better waves to ride into shore, but the tide began taking us out instead of in. We floated in silence, Zoe just a few feet away atop her raft. I don't remember being afraid of the water, how deep it was, or of any creatures below the surface. We had spent a great deal of time at the beach, wading with crabs nipping at our toes and dodging the jellyfish that often floated near the shore.

At some point, two marine lifeguards showed up at our rafts and towed us back to shore. I remember that the one who grabbed my raft had a whistle and his metal ID tag around his neck and was still wearing his khaki green cover. I sat motionless on the raft as he swam me all the way to the beach, where my mother stood waiting in her white-brimmed straw hat and pearl-white sunglasses studded with colored beads, her book in hand. I suspect she yelled at us later, but I don't remember. All I know is that I wasn't afraid of floating out to sea on a ninety-nine-cent raft, and even now, not much scares me.

Grandpa died of a heart attack in his cornfield in 1971, with Queenie at his side. When my mother got the call from my uncle, she fell to her knees in tears below the yellow wall phone in our kitchen. My parents wanted to take all of us back to New Mexico, and the morning after that phone call, we packed our things and readied for the airport—my mom in a dress and heels and my dad in a suit and tie—only to find out that we did not have the $1,500 it would cost for a family of six to fly round trip to Albuquerque. My father bought my mother and brother tickets to Albuquerque and drove me and my sisters back home. My sisters and I cried every day for our mother. We had never spent a day without her.

I wish I could have spent more time with my grandfather. I tried to make up for the loss by spending as much time as I could with Grandma Helen. She lived to be nearly one hundred and wore her wedding ring every day until her fingers became too crooked and swollen. Queenie also lived to old age, leaning to the right when she walked because she had lost her left eye. Some days, we would find her at our small cemetery in Mesita, lying on my grandfather's grave.

CHAPTER 7

The Sound of a Pop-Top

Partway through our time in Virginia Beach, we moved to a house on Aragona Boulevard, and I had to switch schools, but our phone number stayed the same. One day, the phone in our new house rang, and I answered it as my parents had taught me: "Haaland residence. This is Debra speaking." It was my old teacher from the school we'd gone to when we lived on Kenneth Road. "Oh, Debra," she said. "Would you like to be a crossing guard this year at school?"

Strong feelings washed over me. I was overjoyed at first. But when I told my teacher we'd moved and that I would be going to a different school, she apologized and said I couldn't be a crossing guard after all. I burst into tears, and to this day, I can feel the sharpness of that disappointment. I'd never been offered an opportunity to lead, and I think I knew, on some level, that I was yearning for a chance like that. If you're a leader, it's hard to hide. Maybe that's why I finally got tired of my parents telling me what to do.

In 1972, my dad was sent back to Okinawa, and the rest of us moved to Mesita to live with my grandmother. By that time, the federal government had seen fit to grant the pueblo homes indoor plumbing and electricity, and I attended sixth grade at the public school in Laguna. My grandmother would wake us up early and send us out to the bus stop, clothes pressed and hair braided. As a young child, I endeared myself to my grandparents, but living at Mesita for an entire school year was much different from spending only the summer there. I was older, and because my grandfather had passed away, I no longer worked regularly in his field. I felt lost, and that feeling was heightened because I was a bit of an outcast. At my other schools, I had gotten used to being the only Native American in every class, but at Laguna, many of my classmates were Indigenous—when I talked about a kid in class, my grandma would say, "Who's her grandmother?"—and I stood out because my dad was white. Also, all the other kids had known each other since they were babies; I wasn't part of their shared history.

One night, my mother dropped us off at a dance at the village rec center. I joined a group of older people who were drinking beer. I don't remember why I decided to drink that night; I guess because everyone else was doing it, and I was young and impressionable. I don't remember much more, but I was sick that night and the next day.

When my father returned from Okinawa a year later, we moved again—this time to Oceanside, California. We lived in a rental near the back gate area of Marine Corps Base Camp Pendleton before moving into the first house my parents had ever bought, on Redondo Drive. My sisters and I made friends quickly; by that time, we were used to moving and having to start all over again.

I attended Lincoln Junior High School, where the dress code forbade blue jeans, shirts that showed any part of our stomachs, and dresses and skirts whose hems fell short of our fingers when our arms were straight down by our sides. In seventh grade, some friends and I decided that the principal didn't buy our clothes and shouldn't be able to tell us what to wear, so we staged a protest. I snuck out of the house in jeans and a midriff top. By the time our first class started, all the offending girls had been summoned to the office, and I had to call my mom to pick me up. She wasn't happy.

When my dad got home from work that afternoon, he said my punishment would be to wear dresses to school for a month. But I was self-conscious about my legs, so I left the house in the mornings wearing a dress and changed into long pants when I got to school. I eventually had to fess up to violating my dad's edict. When I told him why, he surprised me by saying that he'd had acne as a teenager, so he understood my self-consciousness. He also told me that his order still stood. I wore dresses every day for the rest of the month before gratefully returning to pants.

My dad was soon transferred to Albuquerque, where I attended Wilson Junior High and Highland High School. One of my favorite classes was science with Mr. Montoya. He shared his profound care for the ocean and the earth in a way that held an adolescent's attention. He often told us that the ocean would never become polluted because it was "too big." That was long before someone had the idea of packaging water in single-use plastic bottles. I wonder what Mr. Montoya would think now about the plastic waste depository in the Pacific Ocean that is twice the size of Texas.

In Albuquerque, I began to fall in with a wayward crowd. Perhaps trying to make up for all the times my sisters and older cousins had left me behind, I strived to hang out with older kids. I felt a restlessness that was difficult to explain, even to myself. I seemed to be looking for something that I could not find, and my penchant for a certain amount of disobedience made alcohol alluring when it was around. I had always known the sound of a pop-top, so I invited it in.

I quickly found that drinking numbed my restlessness. It was *something to do.* But what began as a dangerous pastime eventually became a crutch. Over the next decade, alcohol would make me neglect every aspect of my health. I was perpetually sleep deprived, waking up either hungover or still intoxicated. I drank in the mornings to calm my nerves, a habit that only exacerbated my dread and depletion. I was trapped in this cycle, which caused me to ignore my closest relationships, skip family events, and even forget my own siblings' birthdays. I was not proud of these neglectful acts, but their wounding consequences were never enough on their own to make me want to quit drinking.

CHAPTER 8

The Best Bakery in Town

I officially began my working life at fifteen, walking to my part-time job as a salesgirl at Zinn's Bakery every day after school. My sister Zoe had been hired there first, and she came home one evening with news that the bakery was looking for more staff. My parents never gave us money for clothes, shoes, or even shampoo and conditioner, so from the time we were old enough to reason, we had to find ways to earn it. My babysitting jobs weren't enough to pay for the things I wanted, and I knew a steady income would change my life. My starting wage at Zinn's was $1.95 an hour.

Zinn's was in a strip mall on the corner of San Mateo and Kathryn, in the Southeast Heights neighborhood of Albuquerque. A neon sign, operated by a pull cord inside the bakery, protruded from the roof. The pungent smell of yeast or chocolate cake hit you when you opened the door. One bakery case held at least thirty different kinds of cookies, including traditional biscochitos, the official state cookie of New Mexico. Refrigerated cases in the center held layered French pastries, cheesecakes, and other delicacies, and cases on the right had

Danish pastries and coffee cakes. On Fridays, braided and seeded challah cooled on racks. Customers could eat their purchases with coffee or tea at a handful of tables or take them to go in waxed paper bags.

Ed Zinn, who owned the bakery with his wife, Karen, liked to say that he was "born married and went to work in a bakery." He had served in the navy, and he had old-school tattoos up and down his arms and a cigarette perpetually dangling from his lips. His work uniform was white trousers, a white shirt, and a white apron. We salesgirls had uniforms, too: a white shirt, blue skirt, white shoes, and white half-apron that tied around the waist, with two large pockets in front. Each night, I'd find crumbs, price tags, and waxed tissue paper in those pockets. Mr. Zinn came up with nicknames for many of us, calling me Hungry Haaland and one of my coworkers Sticks. He had an answer for any question, and in a battle of wits, he would win every time.

After at least thirty years, he knew everything about the bakery business. One day, I was at the sink in the back washing out cake decorating tubes and tips, and Mr. Zinn was at the wooden bakery bench rolling out a large swath of puff pastry dough with a rolling pin that must have been three feet long and a foot in diameter. The quality of puff pastry, made of flour, butter, and ice water, is determined by how it is rolled. If the dough is made properly, its moisture will evaporate in a hot oven, creating dozens of delicate, lightly browned layers that feel crisp in your mouth. That day, Mr. Zinn was fast and deliberate as usual in his rolling, folding, and turning of the dough. Suddenly, he looked up and said, "This is what separates the men from the boys." I remember being pleased that my boss took so much pride in his work.

Karen Zinn was impressed with my ability to learn fast. Sometimes, while I was working on a task, she would say, "I'm going to make a decorator out of you." I looked forward to graduating from high school and having the opportunity to work full-time in the cake decorating department, which meant more hours, better pay, and the opportunity to learn new skills, but I knew I had a way to go, so I kept my head down and followed instructions.

I had a chance to prove my worth when a customer came in one day to pick up a strawberry whipped cream cake they had ordered. The Zinns were out and for some reason, the cake wasn't ready. I didn't want the customer to leave empty-handed, so without having ever done it, I took it upon myself to decorate the cake. We were the best bakery in town, and it was my job to ensure we lived up to our reputation.

I felt confident that I had learned enough by watching the decorators every day from my place by the telephones, where I tallied the commercial orders—just as I had learned to cook by watching my grandmother. I knew where the cake decorating supplies were and how to split a cake in half lengthwise, fill it with whipped cream and fresh strawberries, and ice it. Mrs. Zinn walked in the door just in time to place the final strawberries on top before I took the finished cake out to the counter. The customer left happy.

I spent most of the money I earned on clothes. One of my first purchases was a pair of brown leather Dingo boots with square toes and brass rings on either side of the ankle. They probably cost me eighty bucks, which felt like the equivalent of three hundred today. Once, my sisters and I pitched in to take Judd clothes shopping for school because he didn't have a job yet. When he was in high school, he mucked out stalls for a friend of our dad's who had horse stables north of Albuquerque. The shovel he used was probably bigger than he was, but my parents would drive him over there on Saturdays, and he'd get to work.

After about a year, I was promoted to managing the part-time shift, ensuring that we all lived up to Zinn's reputation as the best bakery in town. Ed and Karen never asked anyone to do a job they wouldn't do themselves. If a floor needed mopping, Ed would pick up a mop. If we were short a retail salesperson, Karen would wait on customers. Their humility and willingness to do whatever was called for made a lasting impression on me. It was an attitude I've strived to emulate throughout my life and in every job I've ever had.

I was a hard worker, and over time I became one of the Zinns' trusted employees. My sister Denise reminded me recently that the couple even gave me a key to the store when I was still just a teenager ditching school. I'm surprised I graduated from high school at all, but I did. It wasn't that I didn't like school, but other things had captured my attention, mainly smoking pot and drinking beer.

One reason I stayed in school was Mr. Perkins, my senior-year Southwest History teacher. He was brilliant, fascinating, and funny; he would say things in class like "If you really want to embarrass your parents in front of company, pick up your fork and use it to scratch your head at the dinner table." He lectured without notes or a book. He'd put an outline on the board, and we'd all take furious notes, because we never knew what would be on the tests, and spelling was part of our grade. In profile, Mr. Perkins looked rotund, but if you saw him from the back, you'd never know that his turquoise-and-silver concho belt encircled a belly on which he could rest his clasped hands when he spoke. He wore a big silver-and-turquoise watchband and a bolo tie. His gray hair fell bluntly across his forehead in waves, and he would tilt his head back and purse his lips before describing a particular day in history as if he had been there himself, detailing what people wore and what the weather was like. He made history something we could see with our own eyes.

I worked full-time at Zinn's for several months after I graduated high school in the spring of 1978. I'd often arrive at the bakery at 6 or 7 a.m. to find Ed and Karen already there, and I know they kept working long after I was gone. Eventually, a friend of mine moved to California to live with her sister and invited me to join her. I was legally an adult, and I'd never felt readier to leave the home where I seldom felt seen or understood. I was not ready for college, nor had anyone in my life encouraged me to apply, so I followed the Sunset Strip's siren call of billboards and neon lights.

At eighteen, I moved to Studio City and slept on a roll-away bed in the living room until my friend and I could afford an apartment of our own. I found a job at a bakery within walking distance, employing the skills I'd learned at Zinn's. I didn't have a plan other than to earn my way. After moving involuntarily so many times as a child, I knew I could manage whatever challenges I would attract on my pilgrimage from the high desert to the Pacific shoreline.

California was fun at first, but as most addicts know, a change of scenery feels good for only so long if you don't use it as a chance to evolve. At some point, it became my mission each day to earn enough money to buy booze. To have gotten to that place took some effort on my part, and in the process, I wasted a great deal of time. I knew it was wrong, yet I tempted fate every day. The only upside was that I felt the need to make up for all that wasted time by working hard, and that commitment has manifested over and over throughout my life. A couple of years later, I would find myself back in Albuquerque, living at home with my parents and working at Zinn's once more.

The bakery taught me many life lessons. I learned to move fast and make my steps count, as well as the art of the upsell. I also built my muscles lifting large trays of cookies, cakes, and frozen doughnuts that weighed up to thirty pounds each. Some days, I was tasked with inventorying and consolidating the racks and metal cases of baked and unbaked goods, which meant putting on a winter coat and gloves and spending up to an hour in the walk-in freezer. I moved pastries and trays to make room for more cakes and pies and freed up metal sheet pans for more frozen baked goods, some ready for the proofer and then the oven.

In the evenings, Mr. Zinn would "bake off" the pies as necessary in the business's industrial-scale oven. The apple, cherry, and blueberry pies had different kinds of vents on top; the pineapple pies had two holes, the apricot pies had one hole, and the peach had a diamond vent. One evening, I was entrusted with baking off the pies for the commercial orders and the storefront the following day.

You rotated the oven shelves by pressing a lever on the right-hand side of the oven. When Mr. Zinn returned from a delivery and looked at the rack of cooling pies, he asked me if I had taken all the pies out of the oven. I was sure I had, but when he went to the oven and pressed the lever, an entire shelf of hot and very brown pies revolved around to the front of the hot oven. Luckily, they were usable. Instead of getting angry, Mr. Zinn simply asked me to take them out. His small lesson in the art of forgiveness taught me that I am a human being who makes mistakes, a memory that has never left me.

The Zinns often talked about food, and working at the bakery opened my eyes to new ideas about what good food was. Before working there, I had never even eaten real butter because my parents couldn't afford it. When I announced my plans to visit New Orleans, the Zinns gave me a fifty-dollar bill so I could eat at their favorite restaurant, LeRuth's. I went solo, and it was the most elegant and delicious meal I have ever experienced. To this day, I have never been offered a foot cushion at a table as I was at LeRuth's. For a while, I had hoped to attend culinary school, but Creator had different plans for me.

I had finally been made a cake decorator, and I sometimes worked eighteen to twenty-one hours a day during graduation season and ahead of Easter, Christmas, Mother's Day, and Valentine's Day, when the line of customers stretched out the door. These shifts tested my endurance, but I finished each day satisfied that our cakes had made people happy. Everyone worked overtime during holidays, and on the busiest days, Mr. Zinn would get our attention by exclaiming loudly, "We're going to have a sell-sell-sellebration!" In addition to cookies, pastries, and cakes of all kinds, we baked French bread, sourdough bread, and very popular Parker House rolls that often graced dinner tables on special occasions.

The Zinns consistently added equipment and display cases to make their bakery better, including two rotating cases for the storefront where iced and decorated walnut, Black Forest, and Zabaglione Torte cakes twirled on glass shelves. For Valentine's Day, we filled the cases with heart-shaped fresh strawberry and whipped cream cakes; for Easter, we made bunny cakes dusted with pink, yellow, or white coconut, with molded sugar faces and tails.

Mr. and Mrs. Zinn valued their staff. They gave regular raises and bonuses, and they were generous with their knowledge. Some employees had spent their careers there. The Zinns attended our family baptisms, weddings, and funerals, and they stayed in touch long after our final days of work.

At the bakery, I honed my work ethic and began to understand the importance of leadership. I have used the skills the Zinns taught me to bake family wedding cakes, make a living as a single mom, build bridges with staff as a cabinet secretary, and so much more.

CHAPTER 9

Marriage

I met Rich at the Golden Inn, a bar in the village of Golden, New Mexico, east of Albuquerque, where bands played on Sundays. Rich was a welder at Duke City Lumber on Twelfth Street in Albuquerque. He was about five foot ten and thin, with a long ponytail he bound with four or five elastic bands and tattoos all over his arms and back. When he dressed up, he wore heavily starched shirts, blue jeans, and cowboy boots. He'd had three Harleys, and he'd built them all himself.

I don't remember whether I gave him my number or if he came by the bakery while I was working, but he must have asked where I lived, because one Sunday morning around 10 a.m., he showed up at my mom's house. I had the day off and was still asleep. My mom came into my bedroom and said, "Somebody's here to see you." I hurriedly got up, got dressed, washed my face, and found Rich sitting in our living room.

He invited me to see a concert. When I said yes, he pulled out his wallet, which was chained to his belt, and handed me fifty dollars. "Well, then get the tickets," he told me. I was about twenty years old, and I'd never known anyone with money before, so that impressed me. I bought the tickets, and he came and picked me up on his motorcycle. I forget who was playing or where the concert was, but I remember how exciting it was to ride on the back of a Harley.

Rich wasn't college-educated, but he was incredibly smart and witty. He had been born in Florida, but his family had moved to Ohio when he was a kid, and that's where he grew up, the third of four children. His family was drawn to New Mexico by the Indian jewelry industry that had sprung up in the Southwest in the 1970s, when people began hiring Native Americans to make single- and multi-strand turquoise, silver, and shell bead items that were sold wholesale across the country; it seemed to be a fad of sorts. But that jewelry was quite different from the handmade bracelets, pendants, and earrings you would find today in Old Town Albuquerque or being sold by Native American silversmiths under the portico at the Palace of the Governors in Santa Fe. At some point, Rich's eldest brother came to check out the business; instead, he fell in love with New Mexico and convinced his entire family to join him. Their father, an auctioneer who had an antique business in Cleveland, started a similar one in Albuquerque.

Rich came to Albuquerque in his twenties. He had served in the army as a paratrooper, and he was divorced, with three children. By the time we started dating, he was raising his three-year-old and seven-year-old sons on his own. I soon moved in with them. I was young and inexperienced for the work of raising children, but I knew how to cook and clean from my mother and grandmother, so that was a start. I truly loved those boys, and I did my best to make a nice home for them. I taught the oldest how to clean. He was the rare boy who cared how his dresser drawers were organized. You'd take his folded laundry into his bedroom, open a drawer, and find his socks and underwear folded just right. And if he didn't like the way you'd folded something, he would take it out and fold it again himself.

When Rich's oldest son got married at seventeen, I cried through the entire wedding, convinced he was too young and that he and his soon-to-be wife were making a terrible mistake. The next day, his mother signed a release so he could join the army. He ended up serving our country for twenty-five years, and I sure was wrong about his marriage: He and his wife have been married for decades now, and they are wonderful parents and grandparents. Rich's younger son runs a successful antiques business. He, too, was married young, he works hard, and he and his wife have successfully raised four girls. Although Rich's daughter did not live with us, we were all very close, and she also served our country in the air force. I am proud of them all.

Rich eventually quit his welding job, went to auction school himself, and started his own business. I was still working at the bakery, but over time, I helped him when I could. We would drive east to Pennsylvania and Ohio to visit auction houses and antiques malls, buy and load furniture into a forty-foot trailer, and drive it back to Albuquerque to sell. On one trip, we answered an ad from someone selling a square grand piano. Rich was very strong and could move just about anything, but he couldn't budge that piano.

To move a piano, I learned, you must first take off its legs. That means one corner of the piano must be lifted and one leg removed so that the piano can be lowered to the ground and turned on its side and the other legs detached. Moving a square grand piano is not much different from moving a regular grand, except that a square piano has four legs instead of three. Once all the legs are off, you strap the piano onto a piano dolly and wheel it out the door. Because Rich couldn't lift the piano, I suggested using the hydraulic jack we kept in our truck in case of a flat tire. It worked!

Moving furniture was hard. It was just the two of us, Rich up in the trailer and me down on the floor. Those were skills I was grateful to have in the years since. I've had to move alone, and I once carried a queen mattress up a flight of stairs by myself. Sometimes you just have to do what you have to do! I also learned how to strip furniture, paint it, and make simple repairs, and I did a lot of cleaning. Those trips also gave me an appreciation for the craftsmanship that went into building china cabinets, ornate Victorian dressers and beds, and even old barber's chairs. Factories once employed millions of Americans who built the furniture displayed on our auction floor and built it to last.

Rich was funny and direct, and everyone in my family loved him, especially my mom. I was already helping with his business and taking care of his kids, and my relatives started asking if he was ever going to marry me. I didn't know anything about marriage, and my own parents had recently split up after nearly twenty-five years.

I remember the day I found out. That evening, the bakery closed at 6 p.m. as usual, and when I walked outside after my shift, I found my dad standing there. He asked if he could talk to me. At first, I wondered if I was in trouble. We went to a nearby restaurant and ordered coffee, and he told me that he and my mom had decided to get divorced.

I wouldn't say I expected this news, but I wasn't surprised, either. My parents never argued in front of us. If they disagreed about anything, they did so behind closed doors. But I realized that people can grow apart, and we had all been through a great deal as a family. As my father spoke that evening, he didn't blame my mother or himself; he simply said that it was a decision they had made together. He seemed sad, and I understood how, after that long being married, it would be a significant change. I told him I loved him no matter what. Several months later, my siblings and I helped him move to an apartment near the air force base, in the same part of town where we had grown up and where my mom still lived. We helped him put away his things and hang his photos on the walls.

Despite the disintegration of my parents' marriage, marrying Rich seemed to make sense. Even though we didn't always get along, we loved each other, and I adored his kids. My sister Denise made me a pink dress; Zoe volunteered her backyard; my mother's first cousin, Uncle Reggie, offered to officiate; and I baked my own wedding cake. It rained on our tablecloths and decorations, but the sun eventually came out. The following day, we rode Rich's 1954 Harley Panhead to Taos, where we hiked and took a rafting trip down the Rio Grande.

Rich and I continued to work very well together, but at home, our personalities clashed, and we broke up and reconciled several times. At one point, I decided we were done. Rich had recently helped me buy a brand-new beige Camaro. I was making the payments, but the loan was in Rich's name because

I had no credit history. I moved out of his house and took the car with me.

One day not long afterward, Rich came by the bakery and asked if we could talk. When my shift was over, we sat together in the Camaro. "I have to take the car because I don't trust you, and the car's in my name, and I'm afraid you'll wreck it," he told me. I'd had a couple of DWIs by then.

We sat there in silence for a long time before he said, "I've been reading and going to these meetings, and I know what's wrong with you."

He then told me bluntly that I was an alcoholic. Neither I nor any member of my family had ever uttered a word about my alcoholism. Rich had realized something about me that I was afraid to admit to myself.

PART III
WORKING

VOICES

I.

Who would have thought that a drunk like me
would rise above the wet, wet fog.
Go, in a day, from two bottles and a six-pack to clean water
without the Rocky Mountain Spring.

"Booze takes only the weak,"
they say, and the courage I needed was always at the round
    bottom
of an Orange Rock.

I got lucky.
No one showed me the road that goes away and never back.
I only learned it from leaving
from looking up after fifteen years of drunk talk and fighting.

From the gutter there is no place to look but up.
There is no place to look but up.

II.

Who would have thought
a tomato picker like me would rise from the black dirt.

Cracked hands and feet from picking insect-free, blemish-free
tomatoes without personalities for faceless, spoiled Americans
who think tomatoes
come from grocery stores a thousand miles
from my bed of clay.

I never knew no better.
Thought cancer and death was the way everyone lived
until I learned to read labels.

I had to leave some folks behind but they'll forgive me.
They have no choice.

I'm ready now, to return.
To take as many as I can with me. Out of the dirt.
Out of the dirt.

III.

Who would have thought this mixed-blood would figure out
that
two halves do make a whole.

Some people don't think so but I know a full red heart is
better than one empty.

Years spent figuring fractions that never added up.
Years trying to please one side then the other.
Two people in one light brown skin never agree.
So I quit trying.

Instead, I looked toward the center
and away from full bloods with foreign names.

Purity is relevant only
to those who don't see the future.

Thank you, Grandfather, for singing me to sleep.

Thank you, Grandmother,
for the stories of suwimi hanu.
Thank you, Grandfather,
for giving me a past colored in ocean beauty.
Thank you, Grandmother, for your Christian prayers.

Love re-creates. I am whole.
I am whole.

CHAPTER 10

The Twelve Steps

When I decided to get sober, the prospect was both enticing and repellant. I was eager to raise myself from the black hole of physical and mental despair that seemed to define my life, but I didn't know how I would function without alcohol or the friends with whom I'd spent many nights drinking over the previous ten years. I have lived to write this book because I wanted sobriety more than I wanted to stay frozen in time.

Rich was the force behind my truly wanting to get and stay sober, but the truth is I had beaten myself up pretty badly. He approached me with his insight at precisely the right time, when I was ready to hear it from someone who genuinely and deeply cared for me. I was sick and tired of being sick and tired. Rich's sincere intervention tipped the scales, and I finally admitted that I had a problem.

Several years before, I had come across a piece of literature in a waiting room somewhere that asked in bold print, "Are You an Alcoholic?" It offered ten questions, and if you answered yes to at least three of them, the brochure deemed you an alcoholic. I don't know anyone who has ever answered those questions honestly the first, second, or even the third time they were asked. Denial kept me from being honest with myself. Step one of the Alcoholics Anonymous twelve-step program is admitting you are "powerless over alcohol," and step two is coming "to believe that a Power greater than ourselves" can "restore us to sanity." It took me a few days to wrestle with the idea of "sanity," as part of me thought I was perfectly sane—after all, I went to work, paid my bills, and had kept myself alive for nearly two and a half decades. When you surround yourself with people who normalize your struggles, it's hard to see clearly. I surmised that relying on a power greater than myself was the hope I needed to move forward. I surrendered.

With the support of my family, I began a thirty-day inpatient treatment program. I checked myself into a rehab center, where I shared a room with a woman who worked in a hospital and was addicted to prescription drugs. There were about twenty adults in the program, and Mateo, whose family had sent him there because he was abusing heroin, was a bright light to many of us. An amateur cartoon artist who made people laugh, he had a beautiful family who loved him dearly and sometimes joined us for therapy sessions. His wife would show up in her work uniform, and it was clear she was trying hard to hold their family together. Mateo joked that I spent too much time on the phone, and one day he drew a cartoon of me sleeping in a tent near the phone and taped it next to our shared phone in the hall. I kept Mateo in my prayers for a long time because I could see that his wife and children loved him very much and wanted to save their family, which depended on his getting clean.

While at the center, I attended classes, family therapy sessions, and AA meetings, which were held each weekday at 7 a.m. In addition to attending thirty meetings in thirty days, I read no fewer than twenty books on addiction; I read some of them twice. Once I had successfully completed the rehab program, I had to chart my own path. With my Albuquerque-area AA schedule in hand, I went to meetings every day. AA suggests that newcomers find a sponsor to help them work the steps. At my first meeting, I approached a woman and asked her to be my sponsor. I called her every day for some of the simplest things, such as how to fill my time with constructive action, and she was always there to help me.

In meetings, I bonded with others over our past experiences and our need or desire to live sober lives. Every alcoholic likes to think they are special, that their experience is unique, but I came to realize that I was every bit like the people in those rooms. The meetings taught me that honesty cannot be compromised. I readily accepted my position as an average person with average experiences and humbled myself for the work ahead.

The wisdom I began to accumulate helped me understand the role alcohol had played in my life, that I was not responsible for being an alcoholic, but I was responsible for my sobriety. At one meeting, the topic for sharing was "humility," and I stayed quiet. When the chair called on me, I introduced myself and said, "Pass." I did not want to talk. The truth of the matter was that I did not know what the word *humility* meant. Somehow sensing this, one man spoke up. He said that when he first got sober, he thought that humility and being humiliated were the same thing. He gently explained what *humility* meant, noting that although the two words were related, they were not the same. It was humility, he said, that had kept him sober.

Recognizing my humility and being humble have helped me in more ways than I can count. They keep me sober and open to learning because I am sure that I don't know everything. I have to believe that we are all born with this valuable quality, though our society doesn't emphasize humility. On the contrary, most people seem to believe that the bigger the things they can buy or get, the better. Being humble helps us realize we are one piece of a larger universe. My Grandpa Toya, who was intelligent beyond his own perception, was a humble man. He helped many of us see the gift in each day of life, even amid the remnants of colonization and all that came with it. His humility gave him the self-guided mission of lifting those around him and ensuring that they recognized their innate gifts. Thanks to his lessons, I have lived a richer, fuller life.

As a young person, I didn't know myself well enough to understand why I drank. If I thought about it at all, I assumed I was doing it because my friends did. It wasn't until many years after I quit that I clearly saw the pain that had haunted my family and so many others for generations. I lived in the shadow of the terror and loneliness of children taken from their parents, the sorrow of parents who had lost their children, and the larger net cast by federal assimilation policies that lured Native Americans to big cities far from their ancestral homelands—and often to racism, isolation, and desperation. In many Native communities, alcohol was entirely absent before colonization. It was a tool that allowed government agents and businessmen to take land, manipulate outcomes, and undermine Indigenous resistance.

Sobriety was hard, but I'm fortunate that I decided to change my life in my early twenties, when I still had plenty of time to find joy and purpose in making a difference. So much of what I've learned about myself has come with time and patience, and I believe that every experience I've had has made me the person I am today. In the depths of my alcoholism, I lost myself to the constant fear that I was wasting my life. I consistently wished I could go to college, that I could read books and be smarter than I was, but I simply did not know how.

The Big Book of Alcoholics Anonymous implores readers to work the twelve steps; if we follow those steps, we can learn to forgive ourselves, find gratitude, and above all, be happy.

I kept reminding myself that every human is born with a desire to learn, and step by step, I cut a new path forward. As a result of my journey and the obstacles of my own making, I have immense compassion for people who may not have been given the chances I had. I truly believe that, given the right resources and support, many people can live fuller lives free from addiction.

About ten years into my sobriety, I was visiting a sick friend at Lovelace Hospital in Albuquerque when I ran into Mateo. His leg was in a splint, and he was using a wheelchair. A woman I didn't recognize was pushing him around. Overjoyed, I rushed straight to his chair. "Hi, Mateo!" I said, smiling. "It's me, Debra."

He looked through me, without a hint of recognition.

CHAPTER 11

Back to School

One day, when I was getting ready for work at Zinn's, I looked in the mirror and honestly asked myself if I planned to spend the rest of my life decorating cakes. I had been working at the bakery for about a dozen years, but I had always wanted something more, or something different. The next day, I called my sister Denise and asked her how I would go about applying to college at the University of New Mexico. She instructed me to phone the university and ask for an admissions packet. They sent one, and I filled it out by hand with a pen. Part of the process was to get a letter of recommendation. But who on earth would ever believe I could go to college, much less succeed there?

My mother suggested I ask one of her colleagues at the Bureau of Indian Affairs, where she worked in the education department. Laura Garcia is a member of the Acoma Pueblo who believes wholeheartedly in the necessity of education for Native Americans. How else can we compete in the United States, where we make up less than 3 percent of the total population and about 1 percent of undergraduate students? Laura saw a side of me that I never had, and her letter of recommendation exceeded my hopes. I credit her as the first person who believed that higher education was possible for me, in part because she knew that this is our country, too, and that we have an obligation to thrive as our ancestors did. Completing the application was a heavy lift after being out of school for ten years, but I managed to fill out every last form, including scholarship applications from the Laguna Pueblo.

I was nearly twenty-eight years old on my first day at the University of New Mexico. It was there that I began to lead. I learned that when I was passionate and put in the effort, I could gain the support of others to accomplish my goals. I started out as a part-time student because I wanted to do well, and I worried that going to school full-time would be overwhelming. I had a scholarship, but I was also a stepmom to two boys, and I was still helping Rich with his auction business.

When I arrived at UNM, I foolishly thought that college would be like high school, where I rarely studied and still passed my classes, sometimes getting As with minimal effort. My very first Sociology 101 exam woke me up to the fact that I would need to put in a lot more work this time around. The upside was that I fell in love with learning again.

My poor score on the language arts portion of a high school standardized test meant that I was required to take an entry-level essay writing class called English 100. I hadn't realized just how pathetic my writing was until I learned how to construct a proper sentence and use commas. I took full advantage of extra-credit opportunities and attended study groups when they were offered. When my sociology professor implored us to participate in an extra-credit project that involved cooking and serving dinner at a local shelter, I quickly volunteered, considering that I knew how to cook large portions of everything. When we were given a chance in my English 100 class to attend a lecture and write an optional essay about it, I chose a talk delivered by John Echohawk, the first Native American to graduate from the UNM School of Law and founder of the Native American Rights Fund (NARF). Echohawk had also been part of the first class of the Pre-Law Summer Institute, a program that has boosted Native American enrollment in law schools across the country since 1967.

John Echohawk was the first Indian lawyer I had ever seen. He wore a gray three-piece suit, a tie, and cowboy boots, and he had a long braid hanging down the center of his back. He spoke eloquently about the cases NARF was working on, including one that involved returning Native remains housed in American museum basements to their rightful tribes. During the question-and-answer portion, a Navajo PhD student asked Echohawk if he thought she could press the university to let her use English to fulfill her foreign language requirement, given that her first language was Navajo. Her question was a revelation, and I've thought of it often during my years of activism and advocacy. It taught me that whenever we sense injustice, we should ask questions. Action flows from curiosity and our willingness to disrupt the status quo.

Hearing Echohawk speak and, later, taking a political science class taught by former Oklahoma senator Fred Harris made me consider going to law school. Harris had run for president in 1972 and 1976, and his progressive values and slogans like "Take the Rich Off Welfare" inspired me and activated a generation of Americans. I was eager to learn all I could from every professor, and I learned a great deal in Professor Harris's class—including the meaning of the word *acquitted*, which appeared on my first midterm exam. When I saw it on the page, I raised my hand and asked the TA what it meant. The old me might have been too proud or ashamed to ask, but I was committed to being steadfastly honest with myself, and my willingness to ask gave me the opportunity to answer that test question correctly.

I also took a nonfiction writing course taught by David King Dunaway, whose decades-long career as an English professor at the University of New Mexico has been a gift to hundreds of students, including me. The first day of class, Professor Dunaway announced that if any student did not know the difference between *your* and *you're* or *its* and *it's*, we were in the wrong place! I almost backed out, but a fellow classmate told me to stick with the class. Professor Dunaway's opening monologue made me sit up a little straighter, and his personal edits on every paper helped me become a better writer. The following year, I enrolled in a second class with him.

Writing came naturally to me, but when I decided to join the National Honor Society, I was required to attain a certain level in math. I tackled one class but hit a snag on the next. I diligently found a tutor and did many hours of homework every night, yet on each test, I fell short. I shared my frustration with a math-major friend, who told me that students often don't get help at the point in their educational careers when they most need it. Knowing how often I had moved as a child and how many times I'd switched schools, he said it wasn't my fault. I took that as a sign that I could exit my National Honor Society effort without guilt or embarrassment.

During my junior year, I needed more writing credits to complete my degree in English with a concentration in professional writing, so I decided to enroll in a poetry class taught by the distinguished Muscogee writer Joy Harjo. I had never written poetry before, but I'd read Joy's poetry, and it resonated with me. The only catch was that I needed Harjo's permission to get into the class. Figuring I'd take my chances, I showed up at her office unannounced, introduced myself, and explained that I needed credits for the level of English classes she taught. I mentioned that I was from Laguna and that I'd work hard. I was thrilled when she said yes.

I was steeped in my Laguna Pueblo culture, but like any other kid with an American public school education, I had only a faint idea about the history of Indians in other parts of the country. Reading and learning from Native American writers, historians, and even lawyers was both comforting and eye opening. By combining our history with contemporary issues, Joy's poetry captured so much of Indian country's need to be seen and heard. It beckoned me to read other Native poets and writers, whose work I devoured with a yearning to feel understood by writers I had never met in person.

When the poetry course ended, Joy invited me on a road trip to the Returning the Gift Native writers conference at the University of Oklahoma in Norman. I had driven through Oklahoma on family trips, but I had never spent more than a night at a time there. Norman was hot and humid. I had never experienced chiggers before, and the tiny mites embedded in my ankles from traversing the grass in sandals were the worst thing about the trip. The best part was getting to attend readings and performances by some of the most talented and prolific Native American writers in the country. This was the first conference of its kind, and it was very well attended. I remember the audience of seasoned writers laughing delightedly during Luci Tapahonso's reading of "Hills Brothers Coffee" and how her portrayal of the joy and wisdom of our Native elders hit home.

The conference inspired me to write, and I signed up to read my poetry in front of crowds. I realized that I, too, had a voice, and I pledged to submit my work for publication. In my senior year, one of my class assignments was to send a query letter to a publication, pitching a story I had written in class. I was surprised when *New Mexico Magazine* responded that they wanted to see my article. I would have many opportunities to write and publish creative nonfiction about Pueblo life and culture, and I eventually also published a few poems in anthologies, Native American college review publications, and even magazines. I worked hard to get my stories and poems published, and the money I earned from writing helped me survive some of my leanest years.

I had met and stayed in touch with renowned Native Hawaiian American studies professor, writer, and activist Haunani-Kay Trask, and I invited her to give a talk at UNM. When she said yes, I approached nearly every department head, along with several external funders, to ask for the money I needed to bring her to Albuquerque.

Haunani-Kay arrived on campus early on the day of her event. With her bright flowered clothing and long, flowing black hair, she was consistently recognizable, and I saw her as a beacon of cultural representation. That evening, a local Native Hawaiian group showed up before her event to decorate the stage and lectern with fresh flowers and brought leis for Haunani-Kay to wear. She gave a heartfelt lecture on the history and status of Native Hawaiians, relating how their queen Liliʻuokalani had been imprisoned by the US military and noting that the tourist trade in Hawaii was a boon to multinational corporations but a barrier to economic success for many Native Hawaiian people. When a member of the audience asked what they could do to help alleviate this inequity, Haunani-Kay said, "Don't come to Hawai'i. We don't want you there."

I already knew how important it was for Indigenous people to have a say in decisions about their economic development, education, housing, and everything else, but her lecture nevertheless made a deep impression on me. It inspired me to devote my career to ensuring that Native folks had a seat at every table before decisions were made. I remained friends with Haunani-Kay Trask for many years, seeing her from time to time when she visited the mainland. Her unwavering fight for justice for Native Hawaiians showed me what complete dedication to one's people and place looks like on a professional level. When I was secretary of the interior, I got word that Haunani-Kay Trask had passed away, and all I could think of was her lecture that night and how lucky I had been to hear her speak truth to power.

Rich and I were still together on and off, but we wanted different things. I was caught up in my studies and craving freedom. We divorced in 1992. I'd arranged to spend my junior year abroad in Swansea, Wales, and I left Albuquerque as a single person for the first time since my early twenties. I still felt young, and naïve in the true sense of the word. I knew I had a great deal to learn about life and the world. I was grateful when I found a family to live with in Swansea. I rented a small room in their house that had three shelves, a desk and a chair, a wardrobe for my clothes, and a comfortable twin bed, and Marje, Dave, Rhiân, and Ceri became my family away from New Mexico. Marje designated one kitchen cabinet where I kept my food, but soon we ate meals together, and on occasion, I was happy to cook New Mexican chile stew, enchiladas, and even my simple macaroni and tomato soup for them.

MACARONI AND TOMATO SOUP

6 cups water
2 stalks celery, finely diced
1 whole carrot, peeled and finely diced
¼ medium yellow onion, finely chopped
1 tbsp vegetable soup base
8 oz. canned crushed tomatoes or tomato sauce
1 cup dry elbow macaroni
½ tsp oregano
1 tsp red chile powder

In a 4- to 6-quart pot, bring water to boil. Add celery, carrot, and onion and simmer for about 10 minutes, until vegetables are soft but not mushy. Add soup base and tomatoes or sauce and bring to a boil. Add macaroni and remaining ingredients and cook for 6–8 minutes longer or until macaroni is al dente. Serve with saltines or tortillas.

I'd needed to be in an English-speaking country for my year abroad, and the United Kingdom fit the bill. But I chose Wales because Native Americans and Welsh people have similar experiences of oppression and underrepresentation, and the University of Swansea looked like a blend of academia and rich culture. The Welsh people have a strong sense of national pride, which I experienced firsthand when Marje took me to the National Eisteddfod, a festival celebrating Welsh arts, language, and culture. The singing competition opened with the Welsh National Anthem, "Hen Wlad Fy Nhadau," and the entire arena loudly sang in unison. Welsh singers are world renowned, and Tom Jones rises to the top of that list. My mom and I had watched his television show *This Is Tom Jones* every Friday night when we lived on Kenneth Road in Virginia Beach.

Toward the end of my time in Wales, in June 1993, I contacted some relatives in Norway and arranged to visit Skudeneshavn, where my great-grandmother was born, and spend three days on the island of Kvitsøy, my great-grandfather's birthplace and the place where he and his family had lived before moving to the United States. During one of my breaks, I flew to Stavanger and then took a ferry to Skudeneshavn. I stayed with relatives I was meeting for the first time, who spoke generously of our family's history. After several days, I ferried over to Kvitsøy early one morning, and my cousin Jakob, who was also the island's radio tower operator, drove me to the Håland Farm. As we approached, a simple wooden sign on the road directed us to turn left. The white clapboard house was empty, so I peeked through the front windows and imagined, for a moment, my great-grandmother cooking—perhaps in much the same way my Laguna grandma did.

In April 1940, during World War II, Germany invaded and occupied Norway, and Kvitsøy was used as a defensive battery until the end of the war. When I visited decades later, that history was still visible in the concrete bunkers and other military structures in strategic locations around the island. At the radio tower, Jakob let me make a phone call to my mom's house free of charge! As luck would have it, she didn't pick up.

I also made time to travel by rail. On Christmas Eve in 1992, I sang along with congregants during midnight Mass in a small cathedral in Paris. I went skiing in the Swiss Alps and toured castles in Scotland. I had spent my entire childhood traveling back and forth across the United States, and I realized that travel is travel regardless of where we find ourselves. I learned to navigate the hostel system and became adept at packing up each night and finding a new adventure. I was on a train to Pisa, Italy, when a man I had never met said I should go to Florence instead, so I did. I met a woman at an AA meeting there, and even though she spoke no English and I no Italian, we spent a day together perusing the Italian countryside. One of my most cherished memories from that trip was the coffee in Florence. I so looked forward to a cappuccino from the corner shop each morning. I had never known what good coffee was until then.

CHAPTER 12

Somáh

In the last days of my final semester at UNM, I could barely fit behind a desk. I was eight months pregnant, and I knew my final exams might be interrupted by the birth of my child. I went to class each day worrying about whether I would make it to graduation. I was emotionally raw, and I got worked up over the smallest things. I burst into tears when a member of the library staff tried to take a book from my cubicle. Maybe he learned never to tangle with a first-time mom-to-be.

I hadn't exactly planned to get pregnant, but when it happened, I thought, *If I'm going to have a kid, I might as well have one now.* Rich and I were back seeing each other, and he sent me and my belly to Los Angeles to check out some furniture for the auction. I was walking down a street when a man working on a nearby rooftop yelled, "It's gonna be a boy!" My grandmother, who had correctly predicted the sexes of all four of my sister Denise's children, said the same thing. I took their word for it and imagined having a boy, but I wasn't really concerned about my child's sex; I just wanted a healthy baby.

Joy Harjo had become a friend and mentor, and she opened

her home to throw me a baby shower complete with a basketball contest: Whoever got the most baskets from the free-throw line won a prize. Joy asked each of the mothers in the room to tell a birth story. Some were beautiful, some funny. When the talking stick was passed to my auntie Ann, her voice filled with great sorrow as she spoke of the births and deaths of her two baby daughters. Her first child, she said, had a mark on the side of her face that the doctors decided to operate on almost immediately, without asking my auntie's permission. The baby did not survive the surgery. Auntie Ann didn't give details about her second newborn's death.

I had never heard her tell this story, but I was grateful that she chose to share it at my baby shower. All the women in the room grieved with her, and the account confirmed what I had read about deadly biases in maternal and postnatal health care. Through the decades, Native Americans have suffered disproportionately high newborn mortality rates due to inadequate health care systems and a general disdain for our communities. I needed to know that my auntie had experienced abject pain and sorrow at the hands of people who failed to treat her with the same professionalism and respect they would have shown a non-Native woman. My aunt said her greatest regret was that she never got to hold her babies. The attending nurses whisked them away, leaving her to grieve alone.

I felt lucky that I was able to manage my pregnancy on my own terms, and I was grateful that I qualified for Medicaid, which allowed me to choose a midwife. Barbara Pepper was always only a phone call away, and I went to her home office for prenatal checkups. She'd weigh me, monitor the baby's heartbeat, and give me advice about my diet. I continued to exercise, doing everything I could to maintain my health and that of the child growing inside me.

I went into labor two days after I graduated from UNM and spent the next four days having contractions. Barbara Pepper came for a home visit and said I was not ready yet. She told me to stick to my everyday routine as if nothing were happening. I tried that, going to the bank and the grocery store. Every so often, I had to stop, close my eyes, and grit my teeth against the pain. I returned home to wallow in my misery and decided to embrace the process. I was not dilated enough, so Barbara advised me to walk around the house and up and down stairs. My sisters built me stairs out of cinderblocks near the garden wall, and I walked up and down these a hundred times, making sure to drink plenty of water as I climbed. I followed all of Barbara Pepper's advice, trying to decrease the time between my contractions. After my water broke, Barbara felt it was finally time for me to go to the hospital.

My mother, my sisters, and two friends joined me in the delivery room. The moment Somáh was born, Barbara Pepper called out, "It's a girl!" My mom, my sisters, and I all shouted in unison, "A *girl*?" and Somáh opened her mouth and yowled.

Somáh started life with a full head of black hair, but some of it later fell out, and she developed a bald spot on the top of her head like a little old man. I brought her back from the hospital to a guest room at the back of a friend's house on Pueblo Solano Road in Albuquerque, where I was living at the time. I had rented the room while finishing up my BA.

My grandma had taught me that caring for family was

everything. Even though ours was just a two-person family, I wanted Somáh to understand its value. Rich was a big part of our lives then, too. I remember the fear and love in his eyes as he cradled my tiny, helpless infant.

When Somáh was two, we moved into a one-bedroom apartment in an old-fashioned duplex on Wilmoore Drive SE. It was near the UNM arena, or "the Pit," where the Lobos play basketball, and there were baseball and football stadiums on opposite corners. We were so close that on game nights we could hear the football fans roar. The duplex had a gravel driveway and a backyard with a climbing wall, and our landlords lived next door. Somáh and I shared the bedroom; she had her twin bed, and I slept in a double nearby.

I did whatever I could to earn money. I worked as a personal assistant, wrote stories for *New Mexico Magazine*, baked cakes, and ran a casual catering business, cooking buffet meals for events. In 1993, a year before Somáh was born, the Clinton administration had tripled the earned income tax credit, which helped millions of Americans like me raise children as single parents. I was grateful to President Bill Clinton and the Democrats for many things during those years, including the USDA's Special Supplemental Nutrition Program for Women, Infants, and Children, known as WIC. I'd depended on those benefits while I was pregnant, and I later used them to buy baby food and cereal. Somáh took her first steps in the waiting room of the local WIC office in Albuquerque, and the women in the office that day were as thrilled as I was. The staff at the WIC office filmed a series of promotional videos and when they called me to come in and give a testimonial about the program's importance, I gladly obliged.

Every parent thinks their child is extraordinary, and I am no different. I'll never forget the first time Somáh spoke to me in words. She was nine months old, and I was changing her diaper and repeating "I love you" over and over. When I paused, she said the words back to me in her own dialect: "*Ah wab doo.*"

Somáh went through stages when she cried, but mostly she was low-key, quiet, and easy. On her first birthday, I made her a little cake that she could destroy with her hands. I had attended the first birthday parties of my nieces and nephews, and I knew there would be icing everywhere. I put Somáh in her high chair and placed the tiny cake on her tray. All the adults readied their cameras. But instead of demolishing the cake, Somáh sat there calmly looking at her whole extended family staring at her. After a few long moments, she picked off a tiny piece of icing and put it delicately into her mouth. We all erupted with laughter.

From babyhood, Somáh was an excellent communicator. I could tell she was smart, and I knew I had to rise to the occasion. I had read during my pregnancy that a parent should read their child the same book over and over. This way, the child becomes familiar with the words and knows that the outcome will always be the same; this consistency is comforting to a young mind. I had been reading to Somáh like this since she was an infant, switching books every three months or so. But when she began speaking in full sentences, our reading accelerated. By the time she was two, she knew many of those books by heart. She would turn the pages and recite the words, using the pictures as cues. I can't even deliver a stump speech without notes, but when Somáh got older and started acting in plays, she had no trouble memorizing her lines.

My real desire was to instill in Somáh the "sincere interest in learning" that one of my elementary school teachers had noted on a long-ago report card. I had lost that love somewhere along the way before finding it again. Maybe that's why it took me ten years after I got my high school diploma to realize I wanted to go to college.

When Somáh was two, I enrolled her at the Albuquerque Preschool Cooperative, a local institution since 1965. On her first day, she immediately ran outside and got on the swings, and I had to turn my face to hide my tears. She loved everything about the place, especially the teachers and the other kids, but I found it difficult to leave her there at first. I had chosen the school because they accepted nonmonetary payments for part of the tuition, so I was able to lower Somáh's bill by cleaning the classrooms, bathrooms, and kitchen. I was struggling, but I reasoned that Somáh was only young once, and I would do whatever it took to give her a solid foundation. Other parents shared the janitorial duties, and we all spent weekends cleaning up the playground by making small repairs, pulling weeds, trimming, and planting. Somáh and I loved being part of that community.

I had started my own salsa business, and after dropping Somáh off at school, I would get to work. The recipe, which I'd created, included roasted red chile, garlic, onion, tomatoes, oregano, and vinegar, all blended into a smooth, delicious salsa. A Laguna artist designed the label, and among the dozens of New Mexico salsas on the grocery store shelves, my Pueblo Salsa was the only one with an image of a Pueblo Indian village. I built the business by taking my salsa to grocery stores in and around

Albuquerque; on weekends, I'd set up a card table in the salsa aisle and let people try my product. Somáh accompanied me on those outings, and she often helped me make the sale. I would make the rounds of the store, check my inventory, and replace my salsa on the shelves. If I wasn't consistent, my competitors would take up my space. Once I made a delivery, I'd invoice the store and wait for the checks to be sent.

By law, the salsa had to be made in a commercial kitchen, in big, heated vats. I would show up on my allotted day and time with my chile and help with the processing until we were done. A machine would dispense sixteen ounces of salsa into each jar. Then the cooking staff and I would screw on the tops and send the filled jars through the labeling machine, before putting them into boxes with twelve compartments. When a case was full, we would flip the whole thing over, and the heat from the salsa would sterilize and seal the caps. We knew the caps were sealed when they popped, one by one.

I'd then load the salsa into the back of my used GMC Safari van and drive around to stores in Los Lunas, Belen, and Bernalillo, as well as to the Indian Pueblo Cultural Center on Twelfth Street in Albuquerque. I also filled telephone orders from out of town and even out of state, and I made gift boxes and got museum stores to sell the salsa, including one in Washington, DC.

I set out to give Somáh everything I'd wanted as a child. I tried to spoil her with attention. I taught her to love the outdoors as my dad had taught me, packing a picnic lunch before we set out on hikes. I think often about a trip Somáh and I made with our dear friend Alex Harris to Canyon de Chelly, near Chinle, Arizona. There are people living in houses in the canyon, which is jointly managed by the National Park Service and the Navajo Nation. We got a room at the Holiday Inn and woke early the next morning to embrace our adventure. At the Canyon de Chelly National Monument Welcome Center, the ranger encouraged Somáh to take a Junior Ranger worksheet and try to complete the activities while we were in the park. We kept a lookout for birds, plants, and other features of the canyon—as it turned out, the activities were fun for adults, too! We happily turned in the completed worksheet, and Somáh earned her National Park Service Junior Ranger badge.

Once Somáh started school and made friends, she began asking me if we could buy this and go there. When she begged me to take her skiing or to Disneyland, I would always say, "Yes, we can do that sometime," never promising a firm date because I didn't have the heart to tell her we couldn't afford any of it. One day, she asked me if we could buy a hotel. "That would be a great idea!" I told her brightly. We spent hours talking about what it would look like: the pink flamingo wallpaper, the starfish designs on the carpets, the restaurants that served ice-cream sundaes and root beer floats, the rooms with bubble baths and VCRs. Every time she asked if we could talk about our hotel, I said yes. At five years old, Somáh believed our plans were real. This game went on for several years, and although she eventually realized it was a fantasy, I suspect it helped her develop an imagination that served her well in the performing arts.

Determined not to let our slim budget dictate the kind of childhood Somáh had, I sought out every opportunity available to families like ours. She went to day camp and learned to dance because I filled out the applications and stood in line to ensure she got a place. She took tennis lessons one summer because we met some nice people who ran the tennis camp and they invited her to join for free. In second grade, she took after-school Italian lessons funded by the PTA. When an acquaintance gave her a three-quarter-size violin, I found a way to pay for weekly lessons, and Somáh learned to read and play music.

It took time and patience to find these opportunities, but I knew she needed them to discover who she was and what she wanted from life. And I think they paid off. In 2019, when Somáh moved in order to work on film sets in New York, she sent me a photo of her teaching an actor how to properly hold a violin and bow. He was portraying a violinist, and Somáh actually knew how to play, if only the simple tunes she had learned as a child.

When Somáh was four, I decided to apply to graduate school and was thrilled to learn I'd been accepted into UCLA's American Indian Studies MA program. A week before classes were set to start, I was still working, selling as many of my possessions as I could, deciding what would go and what would stay in our move to California. I packed boxes of books and clothes into my maroon GMC van. Rich gave me a thousand dollars to travel with, and I drove out to Los Angeles on my own, the first of many solo trips I would make between New Mexico and California. When I arrived, I checked into a hostel in Venice. Somáh, who was five at the time, had stayed behind with my mother. I planned to send for her when I got settled.

CHAPTER 13

The Big Blue Bus to UCLA

On my first day of classes at UCLA, I picked up a copy of the *Daily Bruin* newspaper and saw an ad for a one-bedroom apartment in exchange for cooking dinner for a family and driving their daughter to acting lessons several times a week. I went for the interview and told the couple that I had a five-year-old. They were concerned about the pool in their backyard; I assured them that Somáh was exceedingly obedient and would not go near the pool if I told her not to.

After calling all my references, Harley and Wendy invited me to cook for them, and Somáh and I were blessed to live in the apartment above their garage in Santa Monica for the next four years. I grocery shopped and cooked. Harley watched what he ate, and their daughter was a vegetarian, so I was sure to include salads, vegetables, and fruit with every meal. Sometimes I would roast a whole chicken; other times I would grill outside.

One evening while I was preparing dinner, Wendy came down to the kitchen and asked me where I had learned to cook. I said I had learned by watching my grandmother. She said that they'd had many previous cooks and that the dinners often fell short, but she liked my cooking. I was pleased that everyone was happy with our exchange.

Somáh was the biggest beneficiary because our address was zoned for Roosevelt Elementary, a California National Blue Ribbon School, where she attended kindergarten through third grade. Her kindergarten teacher had taught at Roosevelt for twenty-six years, and all Somáh's teachers were dedicated and skilled. The other parents were as supportive as the veteran teachers, and we all helped with many fundraising events. Even the dads had formed a group that put on a pancake breakfast once a year. We bought tickets knowing our contribution was going to a good cause. I rode the Number 3 Big Blue Bus to the UCLA campus each day, and Somáh was fortunate to attend after-school programming most weekdays.

One evening soon after we moved in, Somáh showed Wendy her photo album, which included a picture of me shaking Hillary Clinton's hand during her visit to Acoma Pueblo as First Lady in 1999, as part of a tour to promote the Save America's Treasures program. That was a bonding moment for us all, as we realized that our values aligned. I soon learned that Harley had served in the Carter administration and had been a true ally to Indian country when we really needed one. In 1993, Wendy had founded the Children's Partnership, which did quality research for the benefit of children and advocated for health care for every child in California. Both Wendy and Harley are steeped in Democratic politics.

I was proud to have gotten a place in the American Indian Studies program. Professor Dunaway had helped me put my application together, and he read and edited my personal statement and wrote me a letter of recommendation. The campus, with its stone buildings and eucalyptus trees, was beautiful, and I felt at home with the other Native American students. Ours was an interdisciplinary program, so I sometimes had difficulty getting into the classes I needed, like those in history and anthropology, which opened to students in those programs first. In addition to my coursework, I joined the American Indian Graduate Student Association, which put me in charge of fry bread and Indian taco fundraisers.

Living in Santa Monica had other benefits. On any given morning, we would see no fewer than twenty runners on the grassy, tree-lined median near our apartment. One day when I was forty years old, I decided to join them.

I started out running one mile, then two. Getting to three miles was a cause for celebration. One morning, I met our next-door neighbor, a marathon runner, at the backyard gate as I was getting into my car and she was returning from a run. I asked how far she had gone, and she told me six miles. I was astounded. I realized I needed to increase my mileage and that it was possible. Once I got to six miles, I knew I could run ten.

As my runs grew longer and more frequent, physical and mental preparation became more important. One day, I went out in the gusty wind wearing a pair of baggy sweatpants to keep my legs warm, but the loose fabric kept catching as I ran, and I nearly fell. I immediately sought out a book to help me to understand more fully how I should be thinking about running and what to anticipate. I found *Running for Women*, by Olympic gold medalist Joan Benoit Samuelson, a marathon runner who had won a gold medal in 1984, becoming the first women's Olympic marathon champion. After winning the Chicago Marathon in 1985, Samuelson held the fastest marathon time for an American woman for thirty-two years. Her book became my running bible. It told me what to wear, what to eat, how much to drink, and how to manage my menstrual cycle while training. It inspired me to keep going.

On the day I achieved my ten-mile goal, I felt victorious. Afterward, while I stretched in the backyard, I fully inhabited my new identity as a runner. I wasn't fast, and I might not have had the best technique, but I could run ten miles, and that gave me the notion that I could keep going. My collection of running books grew, and I started signing up for races. During one 5K that began at the Los Angeles Coliseum, the race directors highlighted a group of Indigenous Tarahumara runners who wore brown leather sandals along with their traditional clothing. For the first time since I began my running journey while living away from my homelands, I saw runners with whom I identified. Witnessing the Tarahumara runners and racing alongside them encouraged me because running meant more to me than wellness or accomplishment. It was a gift from and a connection to my ancestors.

While I was at UCLA, the Native American activist and spiritual leader Jimi Castillo, whom I came to know as Uncle Jimi, spoke to students about the work he was doing with incarcerated Native American youth. Jimi belonged to the Tongva Indian Nation in California. A marine who had served in Vietnam, he worked as a pastor, mentor, and spiritual adviser to young Native men at the California Youth Authority in Chino. I valued the presentation he gave, and I promised to visit the prison. I filled out all the paperwork and got approved. After my first visit, I reflected that the young men might want to dabble in poetry or need to write a personal statement for a college application someday, as I had. I decided I would offer them a writing class, not unlike the classes I had taken in college, where we read literature and wrote papers.

I went to the prison once a week, traveling fifty miles due east from my house on Georgina Avenue and passing security cameras, heavy steel doors, and metal detectors to reach the small enclave across the campus that was Uncle Jimi's office. I brought stories and poems by authors I liked, and we read and talked and wrote. During one class, I read aloud the poem "El Gato," by Jimmy Santiago Baca, and it resonated with them. They asked if Jimmy could visit the prison, so I set out to meet that irresistible challenge.

I found an email address for Jimmy Santiago Baca online and wrote to him. About a month or so later, and to my surprise, he called me on the phone. After many conversations and requests, and with the help of generous donors, Jimmy Santiago Baca came to the California Youth Authority and gave a week-long poetry workshop. It was the best week I had ever experienced. Jimmy pulled thoughts and words out of my students and motivated them to work hard. On the last day, each student had the opportunity to read for an audience. I think often about those young men and the talent they displayed. I hope that in some small way, I helped them see their value.

The *Daily Bruin* had led me to a safe and comfortable place to live, and I became a faithful reader. While at UCLA, I saw an ad in the paper from a PhD student who was writing her dissertation on the daughters of military officers and looking for people to interview. I called her, and she came to my apartment and spoke to me for about an hour and a half. She asked about pets and moving. I told her we had had to give up many pets and that, one time, we came home from school to find that my mother had given away Bruno, a beloved dog who had traveled all the way from Virginia to California with us. "What did your dad do for his work?" she asked. I remembered a few things, like when he was a drill instructor and we would see him on the parade ground, but I could not answer that question fully. I felt ashamed that after all those years, I didn't know what my dad did for a living, other than that he was a marine.

Afterward, the PhD candidate told me I should not feel inadequate. Most of the military daughters she had interviewed had no idea what their fathers did at work. She recommended the book *Military Brats*, by Mary Edwards Wertsch, which opened my eyes to the social science that had been done on kids raised in military families. I read the book in a day and a half and quickly shared it with my sisters. It made me aware that my struggles with moving every few years, changing schools and friends, and worrying about my dad were family legacy issues that could be overcome. Knowing that my father's military career had had a lasting impact on my life was the puzzle piece I had needed to fully understand where I had been and where I could go. Finally, after working for nearly twenty years to cure my dysfunction, I had found something that made everything else make sense.

I've never forgotten the understanding that experience gave me, all because I'd chosen to answer an ad in a school newspaper. When I have opportunities to speak to students, I always tell them to occasionally lift their heads from their work and look out for open doors.

After two years at UCLA, I finished my coursework for my master's degree. Somáh was flourishing, and we loved Santa Monica, so I decided to stay. I didn't have to pay rent, but I still needed money for everything else. I had pieced together graduate school scholarships, including a few thousand dollars each semester from Laguna Pueblo. I had bugged the tribal government for a few years to create such a thing, and one day, the education director called to give me the good news. After my program concluded, I tutored students in reading at a local charter school, shuttled children back and forth to school, and helped a few seniors get to doctors' appointments and the grocery store each week to cover our household expenses.

Somáh had gravitated toward the performing arts, and I attended every one of her plays and dance recitals. My sister Zoe, who also lived in California, recognized Somáh's gifts and often paid for her theater classes; she even sewed Somáh a poodle skirt for one of her plays. Perhaps best of all, Zoe would join me in watching for hours as Somáh sang and performed the entire catalogue of music videos for ABBA's greatest hits. Somáh wore her share of hand-me-downs from her cousins, but several of my close friends also took her shopping for school clothes every year, which gave her a sense of pride. I remain deeply grateful to the family and friends who helped me raise her.

As usual, I racked my brain for other ways to earn money, and I fell back on my bakery experience. Mr. Zinn used to say that butchers, bakers, and barbers will never be out of a job because people always need meat, bread, and haircuts. I went to Sur La Table in Santa Monica, a fancy cooking store with a demonstration kitchen, and asked the manager if I could offer a cake decorating class there. That led to private events at the homes of wealthy women, where I would bake cakes and prepare frosting ahead of time to bring along. The hostesses would invite their friends, and I'd teach them the basics of cake decorating. Each guest decorated and took home their own cake.

My running became consistent, and in 2003, I signed up to run the L.A. Marathon. I had read that twenty miles would be my longest training run and that on my Saturday long runs, I could increase my distance by only 10 percent each week. I wrote my running schedule on a wall calendar and tried but failed to keep a running log. I ran four to five miles four days a week and did my long runs on Saturdays. I reserved the other two days for yoga, hiking, or lifting weights.

I had heard of the LA Road Runners—anyone could join for a small fee, and the club would get any runner across the finish line of the L.A. Marathon. I showed up one Saturday to find more than a hundred runners gathered and ready to run eleven miles. The long Saturday runs were organized by Pat Connelly, whom everyone called Coach. A thin, elderly man with a crown of thick gray hair and a complete dedication to running, Pat was a former University of Southern California running coach. In addition to the Saturday runs, he oversaw speed training at a high school track one evening a week during the marathon training season. The LA Road Runners had pacers who carried signs, and I joined the 8.5-minute-per-mile group. I continued to show up to Pat Connelly's long runs and faithfully attended his weekly speed training sessions, running around a track and trying to best my previous times with each lap. Coach brought along a partner who yelled out our times from a stopwatch. This would be my first marathon, and I did all I could to ensure that I would finish.

When race day came, I felt ready. At about mile one, we passed a church with a choir on the front steps singing gospel songs. The immense support from the people of Los Angeles who turned out to cheer and distract us from the physical stress and pain of running a marathon—especially after mile twenty—touched me deeply. Along the way, a Native American drum group blessed us with their songs.

Coach had told us that a marathon is divided into two portions: the first twenty miles and the last six. I was elated when I passed the twenty-mile mark and saw him standing there in the middle of the road, smiling, shouting words of encouragement, and giving us all high fives. I had stuck with the program, and I finished my first marathon in 4:24:33.

For two years following my MA program, I stayed busy running, working, and ensuring Somáh had what she needed to thrive. And I continued to cook dinner for my Santa Monica family. I remember waking up one morning and hearing on NPR that airplanes had attacked the World Trade Center. When I walked Somáh to school that day, I exchanged somber words with many of our neighborhood friends. That afternoon, I gathered with other parents, teachers, and administrators at the school to hold hands and sing "America the Beautiful." I had to believe that none of the children understood the gravity of that day, and I knew it was up to me to help Somáh feel safe and keep her optimism.

I had dreamed of becoming a chef, but as I thought more deeply about the best way to help the most people, law school stood out. In the summer of 2002, I studied for and took my Law School Admission Test (LSAT) and filled out applications for UNM, UCLA, Georgetown, Yale, and the University of Arizona. My heart was set on the University of New Mexico, but I included Georgetown and Yale because a friend of Wendy's who was an associate justice on the California Courts of Appeal asked me, "Well, you want to become a US senator or governor, don't you?"

"Sure!" I responded.

In that case, she reasoned, I would need a top-tier legal education. My LSAT score was simply okay, not stellar by any means, but I put great effort into composing my personal statement, and I asked former professors and the lawyers and judges I knew for letters of recommendation. My recommenders all knew me, and their letters assured the law schools that I would have the support of friends and family to complete the three years of coursework.

Georgetown responded first, letting me know that they had 5,000 applications for 525 slots! I immediately crossed Georgetown off my list. I was overjoyed to be accepted to the University of Arizona and UNM. I visited Arizona to cover my bases, but I was ready to go home.

PART IV
ORGANIZING

PERSEVERANCE

Means that I am not going away
That my struggles will be yours
even if you resist

I have stood here in the rain
for as long as it took because I made a promise
to those who led me here
and those who rely on me
to lift their voices into tomorrow

When I knock, you should answer
The world can change
if you add your voice to the chorus
that always rises

An urgency prevails
Earth needs caretakers

The fields are fallow
My people are dying
but no one can hear above the gunshots

The sun will rise once more
and with this new day
hope, for the understanding that will save us all.

CHAPTER 14

Pass the Bill

I moved back to Albuquerque in the early summer of 2003 and rented an apartment on the west side of town. Somáh was nearly ten years old, and I enrolled her in fifth grade at Bandelier, a public elementary school, and immersed myself in my legal education.

I had been accepted to the Pre-Law Summer Institute, which we all called PLSI, and I was eager to begin classes. Housed at the UNM School of Law, the program prepared Native American law students by sending them through an eight-week gauntlet that anticipated their first semester of law school. The curriculum included writing an appellate court brief and arguing a case in moot court. At forty-three, I was among the oldest in the program; many of my classmates had come to law school straight from college. I became a sort of auntie to some of them, inviting them to my house to study and cooking for them. I also helped some of them navigate Albuquerque. I was happy to be a resource.

We had the opportunity to opt into an email chain, so I met many of my classmates online before the program started.

One of the people I met that way was Justin Solimon. He and I were both from Laguna, and we soon discovered that I knew his dad. Justin impressed me by carrying my books to class on our first day, and as it turned out, I needed all the help I could get. Four of the PLSI courses were taught by four different law professors, and they showed no mercy. Their habit of cold-calling on students to identify a holding in a case we had read the night before and explain its reasoning was enough to instill anxiety, if not terror. Our introductory courses on federal Indian law, civil procedure, and torts might as well have been in nuclear physics. When I got back my first Indian Law exam, I was amused to see a D+, and I set out to remedy that dismal outcome as quickly as I could.

PLSI was well worth the time and effort. Those who attended scattered to law schools across the country and around the world, and several, including Justin, went on to become my classmates at UNM School of Law. I'm still in touch with and have served alongside people I met that summer.

When I'd decided to enroll at the UNM School of Law, I ran into an obstacle. Even though the Laguna people were some of the first inhabitants of New Mexico, the University of New Mexico sits on the ancestral homelands of the Tiwa and Tanoan people, and New Mexico tribes contribute dearly to the tax base, the institution charged our people out-of-state tuition if they did not reside in New Mexico for a year prior to attending. This isn't unusual, but it added $18,000 to my first year's tuition. I cringed at the thought of having to work that much longer to pay off my student loans. As I write this book, I am still paying them off!

I decided I would try to make such policies obsolete by pushing for a bill in the state legislature that would change the definition of "resident" in the New Mexico Constitution for the purpose of assessing tuition at colleges and universities. The bill would allow Native American students enrolled in New Mexico tribes to qualify for in-state tuition regardless of their residency. During the 2005 legislative session, I went to the New Mexico State Capitol and visited with Senator Leonard Tsosie, a legislator from Crownpoint, on the Navajo Nation. I described the bill I had in mind and asked if he would champion it. He said it was a good idea and instructed me to visit the Legislative Counsel Service at the capitol building, where they would help me write up the legislation. Senator Tsosie filed it.

When the bill started working its way through various committees, I rallied fellow classmates and even one of my professors to drive the hour to Santa Fe to attend hearings and testify on its behalf. I also testified, telling state legislators that Native Americans never lose their residency within their own tribal communities, no matter where they live, and that New Mexico tribes contribute significantly to the state's general fund through gaming, natural resources, and other revenues. When the bill made it to the senate floor, Senator Tsosie argued that it was a way to fight the "brain drain" by helping Native Americans return home as college students and hopefully stay and contribute to our economy. I will never forget Senator Mary Jane Garcia from Doña Ana County passionately supporting my bill on the senate floor. She and the majority of New Mexico legislators recognized its value and voted to pass it.

Native Americans are the most underrepresented group

in higher education in the United States, and getting the bill passed was my first experience with the workings of the state legislature and the joy of opening up opportunities for marginalized people through policy. It was also a lesson in the degree to which Indigenous perspectives are absent from politics, and a reminder that good ideas should be explored and shared, even if they come from students.

Though I never directly benefitted from the legislation myself, I later met a Navajo woman who had enrolled at UNM School of Law because of the legislation I had helped to pass. She had been adopted as an infant and raised in Los Angeles. Because of the change in the tuition policy, she returned to New Mexico and reconnected with her birth family, and the UNM School of Law gained another Native student who might not have considered enrolling without the benefit of in-state tuition.

As I drove to Santa Fe each day to advocate for my bill, a fire kindled inside me. Sitting in hearing rooms, watching and listening to the lawmakers as they asked questions and spoke among themselves, I wondered whether I could do a job like that. Little did I know that years later, I would become a member of the US Congress and have many opportunities to change people's lives for the better. It's fair to say that the work of getting that bill passed changed my life.

Law school was no different from any other time of my life in that I had to keep working any way I could to support Somáh and myself. Several times during those three years, I was hired to cook for law school events. I would bring all my supplies and ingredients to the school forum early in the morning and plug in my large roasters filled with pinto beans or posole to cook while I was in class. The aromas would waft through the halls and into torts, property law, and contracts classes. At the end of the day, I'd set up my buffet tables and then break it all down after the event was over.

One of my favorite made-up recipes earned our Native American Law Students Association hundreds of dollars at various fundraisers. This recipe calls for one chicken, but I would triple it for big events.

GREEN CHILE CHICKEN POSOLE

1 whole chicken, boiled, deboned, and cubed
32 ounces frozen posole (or fresh posole made from dried white corn)
½ onion, chopped
2 garlic cloves, minced
4 cups homemade chicken stock
2 cups roasted, peeled, chopped New Mexico green chile

You can prepare the chicken and the stock the day before and refrigerate.

Put the posole, onion, and garlic in a 6-quart pot and add the stock and enough water to cover twice. Bring to a boil and simmer until the posole pops, about two hours. Add the prepared chicken and green chile and heat on medium high until the meat and posole are hot. Salt to taste.

Adjust the cooking time according to altitude. Higher altitudes mean longer cooking times.

Enjoy with homemade flour tortillas or Pueblo oven bread. French or Italian bread or store-bought tortillas are good as well.

In my last semester of law school, I enrolled in "clinic." Every law student is required to do clinic before graduating, to get an idea what it's like to help clients with real-life legal issues, while still working under a law professor's supervision. We had a choice between regular clinic or Indian law clinic, and I chose the latter. For the most part, clinic involves a lot of letter writing. People in prison write to the clinic, and students try to help them with issues ranging from complaints about their confinement to problems connecting with family on the outside.

A few weeks into the semester, I got a call from a woman in need of representation at the Laguna Pueblo. She had been charged with eight crimes, and she needed help. I took the case and immediately began to think of all the things I had been taught during the previous two years of law school. I asked for a copy of the Laguna Law and Order Code and compared the wording of the criminal complaint to the code. The prosecutor in the case was seeking confinement for my client, but the woman deserved a fair trial—that right was hers to pursue.

I filed a motion for a jury trial. It was eventually approved, and I defended my client in what turned out to be the first jury trial ever heard in the Laguna Tribal Court. The jury box had been used as a storage area until it was filled with a jury of the woman's peers. I got my client acquitted of four of the eight charges, and she was sentenced to probation for the rest. I stayed in touch with her and saw her change her life's trajectory.

I was proud to send her a designer purse when she graduated from New Mexico State University with a bachelor's degree in criminal justice.

During my law school years, Somáh continued to thrive, and she developed a very special kinship with my professors and fellow students. Between fourth and sixth grade, she spent many afternoons and evenings at the law school while I was in class, and everyone got to know her. Her familiarity with the building helped when I suggested that she wait in a particular location until my class was finished. Whether she was using the computers in the law library, doing her homework outside one of the classrooms, or, per my suggestion, getting in line at whatever random reception was happening in the forum and grabbing herself a plate of food, the law school was a safe place for both of us.

The year before Somáh finished elementary school, I saw a sign outside the Albuquerque Academy campus advertising an open house. The Albuquerque Academy is a private school known for a beautiful campus that makes it look more like a college than a high school. It challenges students with an academically rich environment, offering electives at the time like World Dance and just about any foreign language you might want to learn. Somáh and I both attended the open house and learned of a summer program in which we immediately enrolled her. By the end of the summer, Somáh agreed to take the sixth-grade entrance exam. I filled out the application and financial aid forms, which were very humbling. I had no assets and was not making enough money to pay even a portion of the tuition, but I crossed my fingers and sealed the envelope. A few months later, a letter arrived saying that Somáh had been accepted with a full scholarship. She started there in the fall of 2004 and rose to meet the challenges, even though her elementary school years, like mine, had been marked by frequent moves and many public schools. Somáh knew well what it was like to be the new kid in class.

When I was in my second year of law school, John Kerry ran for president. I liked Kerry's politics, particularly his stances on the environment, but I had another reason to do all I could to get him elected. During our time in Santa Monica, Somáh had landed roles in several student films at the American Film Institute, including Alexandra Kerry's 2004 thesis film, *The Last Full Measure*. We returned to Albuquerque before the film wrapped, and Somáh had to fly back to Los Angeles to complete the final shoot. When the short film, a drama about a young girl whose father is fighting in a faraway war, premiered at a Los Angeles theater, Senator Kerry arrived in a motorcade with sirens and lights. I was impressed that he had taken time out of his busy national campaign during a hard-fought presidential race to support his daughter's film. Somáh and I were both very fond of Alex, and we were proud to support her dad. When Alex came to Albuquerque to campaign, we went to see her, and Somáh was grateful for the reunion.

I volunteered for the Kerry campaign and immersed myself in the work of registering Native voters and getting them to the polls. In the fall of 2004, I saw my former political science professor Fred Harris in the crowd at a Kerry rally at the National Hispanic Cultural Center in Albuquerque. I told him I was enrolled in law school because of the class I'd taken with him nearly a decade before. Professor Harris let on like he remembered me, even though he'd surely taught thousands of students, and I could have been just another face in the crowd. I didn't think that my performance in his class had been memorable, but I took his graciousness in the spirit with which it was intended. Our politics aligned, so I ran into him several more times before we became friends.

I graduated from law school in 2006. By that time, Somáh had spent a vast amount of time playing and doing homework on college campuses and always being the only child in the classroom. When I went up to be hooded on graduation day, I had changed my name card to read "Somáh's Mom," and my classmates gave Somáh the recognition she deserved for being by my side during my three years at the school.

My Constitutional Law professor, Ruth Kovnat, introduced me to Emerge New Mexico, a women's Democratic political leadership training program, and encouraged me to apply to the class of 2007. Emerge New Mexico's parent organization, Emerge America, has helped prepare women to run for public office and show up on ballots across the country; at this writing, there are twenty-seven Emerge state affiliates recruiting and training Democratic women to run for office and helping them across the finish line.

Recruiting women is an important tool in building a political bench, because women often do not see themselves as leaders. As a result, many don't take the first steps toward careers in politics, which means fewer ultimately reach elected office. One statistic I learned at Emerge New Mexico is that when you ask a man to run for office, he says yes the first time, while a woman needs to be asked an average of seven times before saying yes.

If I had waited for someone to ask me to run for office, I would not be writing this book. But sometimes our gut tells us more than anyone else ever will. It can be daunting to put yourself forward, but difficulty should never be a reason not to do something important. I never saw in myself what Professor Kovnat saw in me, but since then, I've always tried to recognize other women's ease at public speaking, extemporaneous thinking, and dedication to community. When I see those qualities in a woman, I feel that it is my job to suggest she apply for Emerge and run for public office.

At Emerge New Mexico, I learned how to canvass, write a stump speech, and make fundraising calls. Many guest lecturers inspired and challenged us. Perhaps most important, the program gave me the tools to effectively campaign for others, and all participants were required to volunteer a certain number of hours for a campaign or political organization. I volunteered for some of my Emerge classmates who were running for office, and I continued to register voters and organize on behalf of the state Democratic Party. I credit Emerge with helping me build my confidence in the early days, when it really mattered, and with giving me a network of women who empower other women to lead.

While in the Emerge family, I was nominated for a national award, but it was up to me to seek votes from friends and strangers alike to secure the honor. Of course, I launched into action and built a campaign, asking folks to go online and cast their virtual ballot for me on the Emerge website. Upon reflection, this could have been a calculated test to see if I could cross the finish line, proving that I had successfully equipped myself with all the skills the program sought to teach. Regardless, it was an excellent exercise in asking for support and hustling on a tight deadline, and when I traveled to San Francisco to accept my award, I greeted both female candidates and my own supporters as the national Emerge America award winner.

Years later, after I had run for lieutenant governor and won my election for state chair of the New Mexico Democratic Party, I received a second Emerge New Mexico award outright. I showed up to the awards dinner to accept my plaque and deliver a speech I'd written myself. Even now, I get nervous before I have to stand behind a lectern. It's something about facing a roomful of people looking directly at me and expecting words of wisdom or inspiration. When I hit the mark, I am grateful.

CHAPTER 15

Indian Country for Obama

I took the New Mexico bar exam for the first time in July 2006. I had studied hard, but success eluded me. I would go on to study for and take the exam twice more. On my third attempt, I was five points away from passing.

To say I was frustrated would be an understatement. As I write this, I distinctly remember my disappointment and the inescapable feeling that I had done all that work for nothing. Without passing the bar exam I couldn't get a law license, and without a law license I couldn't practice law. I came to accept that my prospects for a job as a lawyer had dimmed.

With hindsight, I know that if I hadn't learned to fail and recover, I wouldn't be where I am today. But that failure stung, and it had real-life consequences. I was forty-six years old when I graduated from law school, and like so many other times in my life, I was starting over. I remained passionate about justice, voting, and democratic participation in underrepresented communities, but I also really needed a job that paid well.

You can buy a big bag of beans for very little money and eat them every night, but you can't do that forever, especially when you're raising a child. One year, as Thanksgiving neared, I realized I couldn't afford anything special for the holiday dinner, so I went down to the office of the Supplemental Nutrition Assistance Program (SNAP) and applied for emergency food stamps. When they denied me, I cried right there in the office. I don't remember what we ate that Thanksgiving, but I must have figured something out. I always tried to shield Somáh from our financial difficulties and my anxiety over them. I finally got the benefits we needed, but not until months later, after I'd gone back to the SNAP office and stood in several endless lines.

I got a job as a residential counselor for people with disabilities living in group homes. I also started showing up at the campaign offices of candidates I liked and asking for lists of Native American voters, because I wanted to engage them in the political process. I knew I wanted to continue to lead and serve. I wanted to be like my mother and my grandmother, both of whom had been raised in communities where every member looked out for the others. Like them, I felt a deep responsibility to my state. I knew that underrepresented communities needed a larger voice in our politics. I felt that the best way to achieve that was to organize those communities to vote. I had read about the grassroots effort to get out the Native vote for Democratic US senator Tim Johnson in South Dakota in 2002. On Election Night, everyone had gone to bed thinking the Republican had won, but when votes from Native American precincts were tallied the next morning, they put Senator Johnson over the top. I wanted to do that in New Mexico, because I knew Native Americans deserve elected officials who care about what matters to us.

When I started organizing in New Mexico's Indian country, going door to door was difficult. Many Pueblo homes didn't have house numbers, and there were hardly any street names, either. "Cutting turf"—as organizers call dividing up territory to make walk lists—revealed only a handful of houses, and we knew there were more doors than that to knock. Those of us who worked to get out the Native vote used our creativity. I started setting up voter registration tables at Pueblo feast days and Navajo Nation fairs and asking to attend meetings at the pueblos and Navajo Nation chapter houses.

On a Saturday in one of the pueblos, I knocked on the door of a two-story house and asked if I could talk about the election. They invited me in. It was clearly a multigenerational house, where the aunties, grandpa, children, and uncles were all busy. One of the women was cutting her relatives' hair while the others cooked and cleaned. That sunny fall day, I registered seven people in that house to vote. I shook everyone's hand before I left, and one of the uncles thanked me. "I've always wanted to vote," he said, "but I never knew how."

My work in Indian country has always been rewarding. While knocking doors, I have been invited in to eat and talk about my candidates. At one home, on the Zuni Pueblo, a woman gave me a sack lunch because she didn't want me to go hungry. I have registered four hundred Native Americans to vote in a single weekend; I've even registered hitchhikers I picked up on the side of the road in Indian country. Tribal nations in America have some of the oldest democracies in the world, and as a Pueblo woman and an American, I have a special obligation to maintain that participatory system of government.

Barack Obama's 2008 presidential campaign was the first in New Mexico to put real resources toward Indian country, and I knew it was a valuable opportunity. I volunteered under Lynn Trujillo, a regional field director for the Obama campaign and a citizen of the Sandia Pueblo. Lynn invited us all to a training session at the field office in Bernalillo, and her aunties made a big pot of stew and baked bread. Lynn was a terrific organizer, and she taught me a tremendous amount about how to engage Native communities using the things my own community had taught me. I would load up my car with Native women from Albuquerque and drive out to Laguna or Jemez or Santa Ana Pueblo and canvass homes, finding people who had never shown up on the maps of the voter engagement program we used. We created our own lists and matched them with the voter rolls of those majority-Native precincts, met with tribal leaders and asked them to endorse our candidates, and showed up at village meetings to recruit volunteers and ask if we could post signs. We also cooked green chile stew, baked bread, and invited community members to meetings of our own to encourage voter turnout.

In the years between graduating from Emerge New Mexico's political leadership training and my first campaign, I worked hard for many candidates. I met some amazing people and saw many beautiful sunrises and sunsets across New Mexico when leaving home before dawn to get somewhere or driving on to my next stop at twilight and into the evening. But even though I was surrounded by New Mexicans running for office, it never really occurred to me that I could be a candidate until 2008, when I decided to run for an at-large delegate seat to the Democratic

National Convention. I asked some of my Emerge sisters—or Emergistas, as we say in New Mexico—to help me get elected.

When running for a seat on the delegation to the DNC, a candidate campaigns for the votes of the party's County Central Committee members. They then appeal to State Central Committee members in their congressional district or vie for one of several at-large delegate seats. Even with the party's support, raising enough money to travel to the convention in Denver, stay in a hotel, and pay for food was arduous. As an organizer, I was used to asking people to register and vote, not for money. But I had no choice; I couldn't afford to pay for the trip myself, so I called on friends for donations and joined fellow delegates in selling tickets and doing my share of the cooking for a spaghetti dinner fundraiser at the Plumbers and Pipefitters Local No. 18 in Albuquerque. Soon, I had enough money to cover my trip.

On the first full day of the convention, I walked into a scheduled lunch, took one look around, and immediately backed out the door, saying aloud, "I'm not supposed to be in here!" The room was way too nice: white linen tablecloths, elegant pink-and-white flower centerpieces, gifts at each place setting. New Mexico's state Democratic Party chair at the time, Brian Colón, noticed my panic. "This is for you," he said reassuringly. "You are our delegate."

Brian did a splendid job of ensuring that we delegates had hotel rooms close to the convention venues and an up-to-date schedule, and he booked inspiring speakers for our breakfasts. I also got to meet Native American Democrats from across the country, including Wizi Garriott, who worked for the Obama campaign at the national level. It was the first time I had met a Native American in such an important campaign position. I picked up some Native swag and listened to Native elected officials speak. But my most memorable experience of that convention was greeting Michelle Obama at the airport.

The regional director for the Obama campaign had called the day before to invite me to meet the future First Lady on the tarmac; of course, I said yes. Barack Obama's message of hope and change resonated powerfully with me, and I had worked my heart out in Indian country to ensure he got the nomination. His promises gave us hope that he would be a champion for us all.

When I met Mrs. Obama, I burst into tears. It was the closest I had ever come to a presidential candidate, and I believed wholeheartedly in the candidate I had chosen. The internet has preserved a few videos of that emotional moment, in which I can be seen dabbing my eyes with a tissue every few seconds.

My first national convention was unforgettable for other reasons: Hillary Clinton ceding her delegates to Barack Obama, a wonderful speech by Ambassador Caroline Kennedy, and a rousing, unexpected address by Senator Ted Kennedy, who told the audience that "nothing—nothing—is going to keep me away from this special gathering tonight!" I was receptive to that line because it is always about showing up and meeting people where they are. That is a sacred obligation of public servants, and one I hold dear. When former president Bill Clinton took the stage, the audience roared for what seemed like hours. I had never been in a room with so many people before, and the effect of thousands of Democrats cheering in unison was powerful.

When the evening of Obama's nomination speech arrived,

I wore my traditional Pueblo dress, my black woolen manta, a woven red belt, white buckskin moccasins, and my silver-and-turquoise jewelry. I had procured tickets for my sister Zoe and a friend so they, too, could see history unfurl joyfully before us. When the convention was over, we drove back to Albuquerque, and I kept working hard until Election Day. As the votes rolled in and we watched the returns on the television, I concocted banana splits for my niece and Somáh, who were watching with me. I wanted them to know that some things are worth celebrating.

I was proud when Barack Obama won, especially because Indian country, here in New Mexico and across the country, had helped elect him. After the election, I submitted my résumé, filled out applications, and even sat for a few interviews, but I couldn't find a job with any of the public officeholders I'd worked so hard to elect. I knew I had value, but the truth of the matter was, I was an organizer, not a political operative or a seasoned high-level staffer.

After a month or two, I recognized that it was time to make a new plan, and as one door closed, another opened. My brother, Judd, was recently divorced and raising four children on his own in California. He needed my help.

CHAPTER 16

Auntie Deb

I packed up all our belongings and loaded them into a twenty-six-foot Ryder box truck, and on New Year's Day 2009, Somáh and I drove west on I-40, heading for the coast. I still have no idea why truck rental companies trust their vehicles to people like me, who have no commercial driving experience. It was scary as hell navigating through mountain ranges and tunnels with that big truck and my little car on the trailer behind us, but somehow we made it safely to California.

I had planned for Somáh to stay with Zoe, across the Santa Cruz Mountains from my brother's house, for a few months, to finish ninth grade. Judd's wife had left him, and he was raising their four teenagers while running his construction business. He had been managing the household the way our dad would have: like a military operation. He assigned each kid a night to cook and clean and took one night himself to cover five weeknight dinners; on the weekends, the family grazed. When I got there, I offered to cook for all of them.

I'd spent a lot of time with my sister Denise's children, but Judd's kids lived farther away, and I was grateful for this unexpected chance to get to know them. Judd left the house before dawn some days and got back late, because when you do construction in California, your jobs can be fifty miles apart in any direction. My nieces were curious about cooking, so I gave them lessons. We baked fruit pies almost every night, and I taught them how to make tamales. When my nephew wanted to learn how to iron a dress shirt, I happily showed him. One afternoon, I came home to find my nieces on the couch watching TV, and I sat down with them. "Thank you, Auntie, thank you for cooking for us," they cried out of nowhere, embracing me. I was happy that the meals I prepared meant so much to them, because spending time with them meant the world to me.

In my spare time, I helped Judd with his business. I hired a friend to design a logo and found a graphics company to colorize it. I did a domain search, found a Web address, and used a template to help him set up a website and craft a mission statement. I also helped Judd at work by cleaning up job sites and picking up and delivering supplies; I even learned how to lay floor tile. Judd had learned construction from the ground up. He started as a teenager sweeping floors, and over the years, he worked on every facet of the building process. He could juggle five or six jobs at a time, laying out the work for his people and telling them what he expected. I felt grateful to learn what goes into building a house and what quality construction work looks like.

I also stepped up my running. Judd and his family lived on Aguajito Road, across the street from Jacks Peak Park, which was managed by the County of Monterey. Running on the hills was great, but I could stretch my runs into twelve and fourteen miles by running along the beach and onto a portion of the scenic 17-Mile Drive. Judd and I eventually started training together for the Big Sur Marathon.

Somáh joined me in Carmel that summer, and the following fall, I enrolled her at Monterey High School, where her cousins were students. In California, sophomores are required to take the California High School Exit Examination; Somáh took the test at Monterey High and ranked among a group of students who received the high scores that the school was shooting for. The school administrators were thrilled. I knew that Somáh could achieve whatever she put her mind to, so I always expected her to do well. When she performed exceptionally well in her tenth-grade English class, her teacher invited her on the annual senior class trip to Europe.

The trip was beyond our budget, but I thought it would be good for her to go, so we set out to raise some money. Somáh was an avid photographer; I encouraged her to send letters to everyone we knew, telling them she needed to raise money for the trip and asking if they would accept a print of one of her photos in return for a donation. We sent off the letters, printed the photographs, and waited. Friends and relatives were generous, and Somáh raised about a thousand dollars. Our family pitched in the remainder.

As the trip approached, though, Somáh started to worry. She didn't know any of the other kids because they were seniors, and she was only a sophomore. The day she left, I baked a double batch of chocolate chip cookies. "Hand these out when you get on the bus," I told her, "and everyone will be your friend." Early the following morning, I drove her to the meeting place, and off they went on the bus to the airport. "You were right about the cookies," she told me later.

In the spring of 2010, I got a call from Brian Colón, the former New Mexico Democratic Party chair who had been so kind to me when I was a delegate to the DNC and who had taken the time to build our relationship over the years. Brian had won the nomination for lieutenant governor of New Mexico, and he asked me to come back and work on his campaign and that of his running mate, gubernatorial candidate Diane Denish. The election was that November.

After a year and a half with my California family, I felt ready to go home. I had celebrated some birthdays, spent the holidays, and seen my niece graduate from high school, and I felt grateful. I called Somáh, who was at a summer program at the Institute of American Indian Arts in Santa Fe, to share the news. She told me she missed New Mexico, and together we began planning our return.

CHAPTER 17

No One Knocks Doors in Taos

We moved back to Albuquerque in July 2010, and I dove into the gubernatorial campaign. My job was to get out the Native vote, so I immediately started visiting tribes and scheduling Brian to visit, too. We had just a few months to activate as many Native American voters as we could.

Everything I had learned from Lynn Trujillo in 2008 I put to use in 2010. I found volunteers to help me canvass and deliver signs, cooked food, and invited folks to join us for meet-and-greets with our candidate. We all worked hard because we believed in the ticket. Diane Denish had been an accomplished lieutenant governor, and we knew she would care for our people and work hard for us as governor. But on Election Night, we fell short of the votes we needed. There was nothing to do but start planning for the next election.

Somáh completed her junior and senior years at Albuquerque High School. The school had a wonderful theater program, led by Mr. Ralph Adkins, who had taught drama and stagecraft there for close to a quarter century. Somáh had become an accomplished actor, and she met many talented thespians in that program. I tried to go to every single one of her plays, from Shakespeare's *A Comedy of Errors* to Oscar Wilde's *An Ideal Husband*, and I was impressed and thoroughly entertained each time. The lighting, the costumes, the stage sets, and most important, the students' talent shone through every line, and the stage came alive.

I remained involved with the Democratic Party of New Mexico because I had work to do, and I didn't want to wait until the next election season to keep registering voters. I also worked for a service provider for adults with disabilities, calculating state disability payments, managing client bank accounts, ensuring clients were recertified for Medicaid and that they received the correct Social Security benefits when they needed them. I appreciated the work and found the experience wholly satisfying.

In October 2011, I received an email invitation to a reception at the White House. I thought it was spam, so I transferred it to my Trash folder. The following Monday, I received no fewer than four calls from a number that showed up on my cell phone as "Unknown." I didn't pick up the phone or check my messages until I got home from work. When I finally listened to the voicemails, I found that three were from a man who said he worked at the Office of Public Engagement at the White House. He asked if I had received "the invitation we sent." After looking up his name on the internet, I immediately returned his call.

When he answered the phone, he said that President Obama had invited me to a reception at the White House.

"Why me?" I asked.

The man said that when Obama campaign staff called in to New Mexico to ask who had worked the hardest on the 2008 campaign, more than one person gave them my name. I found it hard to believe that my peers had noticed my hard work, as I hadn't done it for recognition, but because of my twin desires to encourage underrepresented communities to participate in our political process and to help our candidates win.

After the call, and still a little skeptical, I retrieved the invitation from my Trash folder and read through it. Although it was electronic, it was a lovely invitation. Had it been on paper, the lettering and presidential seal would have been in gold leaf. I called my sister to see what she thought.

"You need to go!" Zoe said.

I realized that this was a once-in-a-lifetime experience, so I bought plane tickets for myself and Somáh on my credit card.

I had been to the White House with my mom and siblings when I was a child, back when anyone could drive up, park, and take a tour. I was proud to be invited back by the first African American president. Somáh and I went to Washington, DC, slept on my friend Alex Harris's couch, and met President Obama at the White House. I met many other guests at the reception who were dedicated to our country and our democracy. Some were judges, some business owners; I was just a single mom who had volunteered.

During Obama's reelection campaign in 2012, I asked to volunteer again. I helped out for several weeks, and when a few full-time positions opened up, I applied. I interviewed with Pam Coleman, who had welcomed me as a volunteer several weeks earlier. About thirty minutes into our meeting, she asked if I would be willing to work for a week on a trial basis, so they could evaluate my performance.

"For free?" I asked.

Pam said yes.

I wanted to help get Obama reelected, so I joined the team, working without pay for the first week and doing all I could to prove my value until I was hired as a regional field director, or RFD. I worked in Valencia County, in Rio Rancho, and in Albuquerque's Southeast Heights and Westside. I later became the campaign's Native American vote director for New Mexico and opened field offices in Taos and Gallup.

Before making my first trip to Taos for the campaign, I called around to lay the groundwork for our event—an ice-cream social at the end of Taos's July 4 parade. One person I called was Helen South, a reliable Democrat in Taos County with a stellar voting record and evidence of county party support. She was also a strong Obama supporter, and before the conversation ended, she had invited me to stay at her house while I was there. I planned to be in Taos for at least a few months, and I gratefully accepted Helen's invitation. She was generous and welcoming, and as time went on, we became friends. I'd come home late at night to find that she'd kept a light on and dinner warm for me in the oven.

As regional field director, I was responsible for opening our joint office in Taos with the county Democratic Party and getting it in working order. I gathered volunteers to help clean the floors, windows, and bathrooms and trim the hedges outside. It was hard work, but I knew how to do that. Soon, we had volunteers in the office making calls and helping to plan upcoming events. George Brown, an invaluable volunteer, was great at inputting our data, and he gathered all the call sheets and marked who had gotten calls and the results. I spent many late nights at George and his wife Reggie's house, using their internet. They would go to bed, and I would let myself out.

When I began organizing in Taos, I printed out my walk lists and just started knocking on doors. At one of the first houses I visited, a woman who answered the door said with surprise, "No one knocks doors in Taos!" Taos County is reliably blue, but I've always felt that everyone deserves a chance to engage with our campaigns, and I wanted to share with voters my reasons for supporting our Democratic candidates: because they wanted everyone to have health insurance and they cared about the environment, to name a few. So I took it upon myself to canvass homes in every neighborhood in the town of Taos.

Taos is beautiful in the summer, its trees heavy with ripe peaches and apples. At one house, a large, old tree dotted with muted-red apples about the size of golf balls graced the front yard. Many apples were scattered on the ground beneath the branches, and the owner told me her mom used to jar the apples with the leaf and stem intact. Those jars of apples were something to behold, she told me, before handing me a paper bag and inviting me to help myself. I surmised that it was Creator's intention to feed me while in Taos, and I have loved the town and the Pueblo of Taos ever since.

One day at Taos Pueblo, I met a grandma sitting on her front porch. I made small talk for a while, and she told me that she always votes. I thanked her and asked her if she would vote for President Obama for reelection. She brushed her right hand against her left forearm and said, "I like President Obama. He looks like me." She assured me that she would vote for him. That was my last house in Taos Pueblo that day, and I left feeling that my work there was important in helping this small community be seen.

My own relatives were harder to convince. My parents were lifelong Republicans. My dad's allegiance likely stemmed from his military service. My mother told me that when they lived in the Indian Camp in Winslow, a Republican came around to register all the Indians. Her entire family registered as Republicans. I believe this family history was why my mom refused to vote for Obama in 2008 or 2012.

I had better luck with Auntie Ann. When I called every election year to ask her to vote for Democrats, all she would say was "Grandpa was a Republican all his life." That excuse never sat well with me, as it was a new era in politics, and the Republicans just didn't identify with the struggles and problems facing Indian country. I did my best to highlight this every time we spoke, armed with present-day examples. I mentioned to my aunt that President Obama was the best president Indian country had ever had; that he had worked hard to settle the *Cobell* case, which had started with a federal employee questioning the accounting of Indian trust monies. I also mentioned the Affordable Care Act and that Native Americans enjoyed expanded health care access because of it. Finally, in October 2012, Auntie Ann called to tell me that she had decided to vote for Obama.

Surprised, I asked why.

"He went to visit his grandma when she was sick," Auntie Ann replied. "He cares about his family, and I want a president like that."

I told her I agreed and that I was voting for him for the same reasons.

The 2012 election cycle was Somáh's entry into Democratic politics. Although she had accompanied me on some of my canvassing rounds, she was not yet independent of my political activities. But when two organizers from the campaign went to Albuquerque High School in the hope of recruiting student volunteers, Somáh raised her hand. She and several friends formed a group called Bulldogs for Obama, a nod to their Albuquerque High School mascot. Suddenly, it became the cool thing to bring all her friends to the campaign office, where she and a cohort of blissful, excited teenagers made thousands of calls per day.

Somáh was a senior in high school that year, and I'd enrolled her in an SAT/ACT prep course that started at eight o'clock on Saturday mornings and lasted most of the day. I know that was a lot to ask of a teenager, but Somáh woke up at seven on those Saturdays and dutifully went off to class. Because I was working hard for the Obama campaign and often on the road, I asked my dear friend Suzanne to help Somáh with her college applications. Suzanne had a PhD, and I trusted her in this realm more than I trusted myself. Somáh would go over to Suzanne's house a couple of times a week, and they would work on her personal statement.

When she was choosing where to apply, I encouraged Somáh to cast a wide net. I urged her to apply to Dartmouth, which had recommitted to educating Native Americans and had created an excellent program. I also thought that a few University of California schools would suit her, but Somáh could be stubborn, and she said she didn't want to go to school in New Hampshire or California.

The Saturday morning classes paid off, and she aced her standardized tests. Her scores caught the attention of many schools, including the University of New Mexico. A letter soon arrived in the mail from UNM saying that Somáh had been recognized as a National Native American Scholar and that they wanted to offer her a four-year scholarship.

"Do you really want to pay for college?" she asked when she showed me the letter. "Or do you want me to go here for free?"

There wasn't much I could say to that. She'd made her case for staying in Albuquerque.

That summer, the Obama campaign organized a Pride event that Somáh and I attended. As we were getting ready to open the doors, Pam Coleman, the campaign's field director at the time and my boss, noted Somáh's participation and asked, "How does it feel to be the mom of a gay child?"

"It feels fine," I said immediately, trying to keep my surprise from showing. It was news to me, but I didn't want to ask, "Is Somáh gay?"

When we got home that night, I looked searchingly at Somáh. "Why didn't you tell me you were gay?" I asked.

"Why should I have to tell you that?" she replied without hesitation. "Do heterosexual kids sit their parents down to tell them they're straight?"

I didn't know what to say. "Probably not," I sheepishly agreed.

"Well, why do I have to tell you I'm gay?"

"You don't," I replied. "But I'm just saying, I wish I had known. I didn't know."

I'm grateful that Somáh has always been powerfully honest about who she is. I recently found an old photo of her dressed in a secondhand ribbon shirt, rainbow suspenders, laced cowboy boots, and tiny Wrangler jeans, with her beautiful curly hair framing a broad smile. She was only about four years old at the time, but it was a classic look for a child who would become nonbinary. I had been a proud ally of the LGBTQ+ community for many years before learning that Somáh was a part of that community herself, but after that conversation, I felt an even greater obligation to do all I could. I needed to protect my child's future in every way possible.

When Somáh graduated from high school, I thought, *There's no way I'm not celebrating this.* Although my job with the Obama campaign was the first I'd ever had that came with health insurance, money was very tight. I cleared about three thousand dollars per month after taxes, and I didn't know how I would come up with enough to throw Somáh a decent party. After turning it over in my head for a while, I drove to a payday lender in Albuquerque and borrowed money, using my car as collateral. The deal scared me. I had never borrowed money before, other than a few hundred dollars from family members. I had about a month to pay off the loan in full at little cost, but after that, the payments would become exorbitant.

I didn't think I had a choice; after all that Somáh had endured as my child—moving, repeatedly going to new schools, and wearing hand-me-downs and thrift store clothes her entire life up to then, she deserved recognition for her accomplishment. It took me a year to pay off the loan, and I never told anybody, not even my family. It was excruciating, but the party was worth every penny. Family and friends came to celebrate at the Indian Pueblo Cultural Center, and I made Somáh a cake in the shape of an open book, which I decorated to look like *The Importance of Being Earnest*. It was a hit.

That spring, I encouraged Somáh to run for a delegate seat at the 2012 Democratic National Convention. She put up a bit of a fuss over all the phone calls and the writing of postcards to State Central Committee members. And I repeated what I'd often told her when the work got tough: "You will thank me." When the day came to elect delegates to the convention, Somáh recruited a few high school classmates to hold up signs and talk to voters on her behalf at the State Central Committee meeting.

Somáh was selected as a delegate, and in September she attended the 2012 Democratic National Convention held in Charlotte, North Carolina. We stayed in touch throughout the week. About halfway through Bill Clinton's speech, I received a text from her that read simply, "Thank you, Mommy." Somáh got a great deal of attention as the youngest LGBTQ+ delegate, and I was proud she had worked so hard to get there.

Throughout the 2012 Obama campaign, all staff were required to turn in nightly reports. I often worked late, sometimes not filing my reports until 2 a.m. I assured my state director that I could survive on little sleep. I had always done so.

He was not pleased. "That is not sustainable!" he scolded. Because of me, he made a new rule that all nightly reports had to be turned in by 11 p.m.

I remained committed to my job and kept working late. On Election Night, when we far exceeded our voter goals in Indian country and Obama won the presidency for a second time, I texted my former state director, who had left the campaign but who remains a friend to this day, "It was sustainable after all!"

PART V
RUNNING

AN OCEAN OF TEARS SEEMS ENOUGH

to cry, for anything beautiful.
Simply to express love, but more
to ensure its eternity.

If I were to meet with turtle today,
he'd offer wisdom
on living slow and without objection.
He'd say: "Take my home."
and tell me to guard it well,
while he rests for a while.
His load is unbearable
at times, but he forever moves with grace and pity,
the way my grandmother once did.
We could all die with a look of peace.

To share
victories

hardships
disdain, and
Love is the way of the current
carrying the turtle to his next destination.
We should, together, carry weight on our backs
and always leave room for certain hearts.

That beauty would be enough.

CHAPTER 18

Showing Up

The Pueblo Indians have an enduring cultural tradition of running. Before motorized vehicles and even horses and wagons, if a person wanted to get somewhere, they did so on foot. If they wanted to get somewhere faster, they got there by running. The Pueblo Revolt of 1680 succeeded because runners traversed many hundreds of miles to each and every pueblo in the Southwest to deliver knotted yucca ropes relaying instructions from the great Pueblo leader Po'pay to untie a knot each day leading up to their organized rebellion. I once read that, in his youth, the Hopi Olympic medalist Lewis Tewanima would run over fifty miles from his home village of Shongopovi to Winslow just to watch the trains pass, then turn around and run the fifty-plus miles back.

Ever since I was a young girl, I've known people who ran. My grandpa Lucas from Jemez, Grandpa Toya's brother-in-law, ran the Pikes Peak Ascent many times and had the trophies to prove it. But I had not considered that the ancestral tradition of Pueblo runners also resided in me. That changed years ago in Santa Monica when I laced up my sneakers, craving the sensation of hard earth beneath my feet. I feel most connected to the earth when I am running on it.

Deciding to run for my first elected office was similarly intertwined with my heritage. In 2013, I became a tribal administrator for a New Mexico tribal government. I was grateful to be of service to the community, overseeing tribal programs and ensuring I was attentive to tribal leadership. It was also the best-paying job I had ever had. The role reminded me that I could make a positive difference for people, and my colleagues there became like family to me.

The following year, feeling that the New Mexico Democrats needed a fresh candidate, I considered running for lieutenant governor. I had spent years organizing in Indian country, and I thought I could inspire even more of my people to vote than had turned out for Obama. That was an outsize idea considering that it was a midterm election and the incumbent Republican governor had a massive war chest. Nonetheless, I remained optimistic. One day, my friend Scott Tillman called out of the blue. "Why do people keep telling me that you're running for lieutenant governor?" he asked. It seemed that word was getting around. I felt strongly that the Democrats deserved a lieutenant governor candidate who worked hard and cared about the people of New Mexico, and I decided to plunge ahead.

What followed was a crash course in candidacy: I wrote my own speeches, did my own interview prep, mapped out campaign stops and travel, knocked doors, made phone calls, and fundraised. Thanks to the political leadership training I'd received from Emerge New Mexico, I had the basics down, but the real thing is faster-paced and more serious than anything I could have imagined. Suddenly, everything I said found a way onto social media, and people were paying attention. As the days passed, I realized I really did have a knack for campaign life. I find my greatest joy when I can meet new people, roll up my sleeves, and get to work. My time at the bakery prepared me well to endure long hours, and my organizing years were the perfect training for the scrappy campaign we had to run. During the general election, I found someone to drive me around the state, and that was a lifesaver. I had retained my seat on the Laguna Development Corporation Board of Directors and was still working my tribal administrator job—until about a month and a half before Election Day, when I asked for a leave of absence.

Up to that point, I had been the main caretaker for Somáh's cat, Basil Basildon. But one night during the campaign, I came home to find Basil gone and a dog in his place! He was a medium-size brown mutt with a white chest and paws. I had grown up with dogs, so I was happy to have him around, though campaign hours can be very long, and he didn't seem suited to extended periods alone. We named him Remington, and I made sure he had shade outside, a comfortable place to sleep, and plenty of food and water, but when I'd come home late at night, he would cry in my arms for several minutes before he calmed down. I decided he needed a sister, and I found him a rez dog at the Laguna tribal building, a stray seven-month-old puppy whom Somáh named Winchester—Winnie, for short. We were one big, happy family!

I was nervous giving stump speeches, so I wrote my thoughts on index cards and flipped through them as I spoke. During our preprimary convention sweep, I gave many speeches throughout New Mexico's thirty-three counties, and with practice, I grew more comfortable. I still do this, starting with cards and rough drafts and fine-tuning as I learn from people and hear more about the issues they care about.

I made many trips to Laguna Pueblo during that campaign, and I often visited my mom in Mesita. One summer day, she told me she was excited to vote for me in the primary. I responded that she couldn't, because she was a registered Republican. There was a long pause. "Well, okay," she said. I quickly produced a voter registration form and registered her as a Democrat.

I won the primary, but the general election proved tougher. Our gubernatorial nominee, Gary King, was New Mexico's attorney general. He had a strong platform on education and equity for working people, and his father, Bruce King, had been a rancher and beloved three-time governor. But we were up against the incumbent Republican, Susana Martinez, a longtime prosecutor who had beaten Diane Denish and Brian Colón in the 2010 statewide campaign I had worked on. She ultimately raised seven million dollars for her reelection, and her campaign spent much of it on ads that demonized her political enemies and presented her as a caring leader. In reality, she had decimated our behavioral health system by withholding payments to organizations that provided such care for many low-income New Mexicans. She had accused them of fraud, and it took years for the attorney general to clear the providers of wrongdoing. By that time, many had shut down, and tens of thousands of New Mexicans suffered as a result.

Gary and I were proud when New Mexican labor icon

Dolores Huerta, who cofounded the National Farm Workers Association, returned to her birthplace to join us on a bus tour. The tour's last stop was the state Democratic Party headquarters, where we alighted from the bus to a cheering crowd. One weekend shortly before the election, Gary and I joined several other Democratic candidates at a classic Las Vegas restaurant called Charlie's Spic and Span in Northern New Mexico's San Miguel County. Part of my job was to introduce Gary to the crowd of about 150 people at the restaurant. "You have heard many people say this is a historic election," I told them. "If Gary and I win, I will be the first Native American to hold a statewide office in New Mexico!" The audience cheered and clapped. "But this election is historic for another reason," I went on. "If Gary and I win, it will be the first time a cowboy and an Indian will run the state government together!" The crowd went wild. That was a turning point—I felt a burst of giddy confidence as I realized that I could successfully go off script.

Another time, I drove to Roy, a tiny village in Northern New Mexico, for a Harding County "Hamburger Fry." My sister Denise's husband, Scott, is from Roy. His grandmother's family, the Coles, came to New Mexico in a covered wagon from Oklahoma when she was two years old. Her family lived in a dugout until they could build a proper home in Roy. On Scott's father's side, the Kirkseys settled near the deep canyon cut by the Canadian River coming out of the Rocky Mountains in Northern New Mexico. Many New Mexicans have similar stories, and as I traveled the state, I was constantly reminded why we are so invested in our future. In a place like Roy, the land goes on forever, and the sky does, too. Its residents have been there for many generations, and they want to stay there for the benefit of their children and grandchildren.

Denise and Scott drove from their home in Clayton, New Mexico, to join me at the Hamburger Fry, where candidates were invited to stump for support. Two women running for the same local office spoke one after the other. The second candidate talked about what she would do for Harding County, then looked at the first candidate and said, "You won for prom queen back in high school, and now it's my turn!" Everyone laughed, of course.

Afterward, we decided to go for a drive to check on Scott's parents' property. Roy is a quintessential southwestern town whose main street could be a setting for a Taylor Sheridan Western. As we drove down streets named for US presidents—Roosevelt, Taft, McKinley—Denise looked up and blurted out, "That's Roe!" Roe, her son's dog, had run away two years before. Apparently, she had made it one hundred miles from Clayton to Roy and found her way to someone else's home. Denise knocked on the door of a white stucco, pitched-roof house with a generous front porch. The woman who answered the door said that she took in whatever dogs showed up. Denise bundled Roe into the car, and my nephew got his dog back.

In spite of our hope and hard work, the 2014 election was a washout. Many voters would say that Democrats didn't put their best foot forward, but as the lieutenant governor nominee, it was my job to invite voter enthusiasm, and no matter what, running against an incumbent is nearly always an uphill slog. We lost the governor's race, and our statehouse went to Republicans after more than fifty years of Democratic control, although Demo-

My dad with the catch of the day, circa 1944. His family's farm in New London, Minnesota, was located on Nest Lake, and my father learned to fish at an early age, and he in turn taught me how to bait a hook. He loved the water and was always ready to cast his line. *(Courtesy of the author)*

My father, always an optimist, wanting to move this bull in his direction. In this family photo, he looks to be around five years old (circa 1941) and is on the farm in New London. *(Courtesy of the author)*

I couldn't say for sure, but my father may be at his barracks on a military base in Southern California. He was a proud US Marine all of his career, and he was respected by his troops and fellow brass alike. My family loved him for it. Circa mid- to late 1950s. *(Courtesy of the author)*

In 1953, the Santa Fe All-Indian Band was invited to play in President Eisenhower's inaugural parade. My mother told me that the band alighted at train depots along the route from Winslow, Arizona, to Washington, DC, to play mini-concerts for passersby. Here they are at the Albuquerque train depot. *(Courtesy of the author)*

Grandpa Conrad, Grandma Mae Haaland, and my dad, Dave Haaland, in San Francisco. Circa 1950. *(Courtesy of the author)*

Circa late 1950s—I can tell because my mother is wearing her wedding ring, and she and my dad married in 1956. My grandpa, Tony Toya, in his classic fedora and rolled sleeves, and my mom appreciating a district championship trophy won by the Winslow Redskins baseball team, which he founded.

(Courtesy of the author)

On baking day, my grandma always wrapped her hair. Here we are at her mud oven in Winslow, Arizona, the same mud oven where I watched diligently to absorb all of my grandma's cooking rituals. From left: my grandma, Zoe, me, Denise, my cousin Georgia, and my grandpa in his ubiquitous railroad cap. *(© Mary Toya)*

Zoe, Dutch Haaland, me, Denise, and Judd in the front. On Saturday, March 7, 1970, a solar eclipse occurred, and we stayed out all day waiting for it at the behest of my dad. As a mom, I always searched for ways to spark curiosity in Somáh the way my dad did in me. Virginia Beach, Virginia. *(© Mary Toya)*

My mom and me, nine months pregnant with Somáh, on UNM graduation day, May 1994. *(© Zoe Magee)*

Somáh's first trip to the Grand Canyon. In 1995, Marje Tanner came to visit me from Swansea, Wales. She, Somáh, and I set out on a road trip from Albuquerque to California to see my sister Zoe, and we stopped at the Grand Canyon. *(© Marje Tanner)*

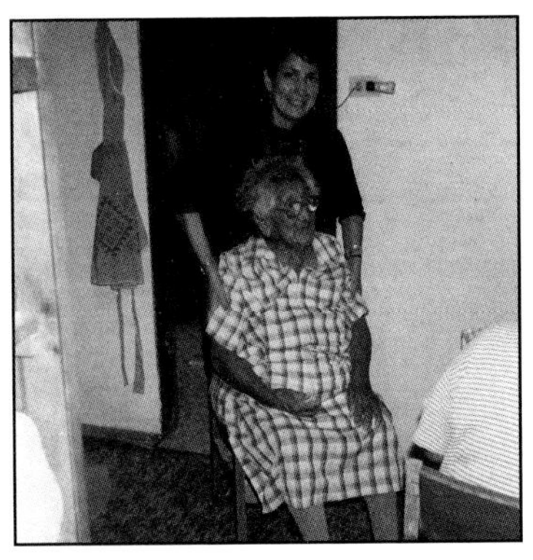

My grandma, having hung up her apron for the day, taking a rest after cooking and getting a shoulder rub from me. This photo was likely taken in the early 1990s at her home in Mesita Village. *(Courtesy of the author)*

Pojoaque Pueblo hosted a piki-making class at the Poeh Cultural Center in the early 2000s. The piki is a blue corn bread with a sweet flavor and flaky texture, and is always a treat when it is served in a family home.

(Courtesy of the author)

Marching on Cesar Chavez Day, 2019, in the Barelas neighborhood of Albuquerque. I walked in the parade with Dolores Huerta, whom I have come to know personally and admire greatly as a woman who continues to build change in her community and uses her influence to make people's lives better.

(© Israel Chávez)

Crossing the Edmund Pettus Bridge with colleagues and friends during the Faith and Politics Tour in Alabama, 2019. I remember the overwhelming feeling of significance and profound gratitude as my steps moved across that bridge. That year was the last time the Hon. John Lewis did this march. From left, Congresswomen Kendra Horn, Lisa Blunt Rochester (now a US senator), me, and Veronica Escobar. *(© Jennifer Van der Heide)*

Showing off my transgender flag at Longworth House Office Building, 2019. I was the first congressmember in history to display this flag at my office. *(Courtesy of the author)*

I would train for my upcoming races in the mornings before heading to my first meetings of the day serving New Mexico's first congressional district. Here I'm training for the Army Ten-Miler in October 2019. *(© Christopher Garcia)*

In my "limo" that would be my home for the next four years. I was on the way to the White House to get sworn in as secretary of the interior. *(© Skip Sayre)*

One of the first actions I took as secretary of the interior was to work to remove all derogatory place names from the federal lands that the Department of the Interior managed. We traveled to Alcatraz Island, a National Park Service unit, to give a speech on this action and to pay respects to the struggle of Indigenous peoples. November 2021. *(© Heather Barmore)*

An official trip to Chaco Culture National Historical Park. While in Congress, I worked on a bill to protect Chaco, and while I was at the Department of the Interior we were successful in withdrawing a ten-mile radius from around the unit to protect it from extraction. November 2021.

(© Heidi Todacheene)

I traveled to the Cherokee Nation in Oklahoma with the First Lady, Dr. Jill Biden, to highlight our work on Native language revitalization. We made a stop on the way back and I took the opportunity for a photo in front of her plane. December 2021.

(© Melissa Schwartz)

Giving my speech during the event when President Joe Biden offered a national apology to Indian country regarding the federal Indian Boarding School era. It was a full circle moment on an endeavor I had first set out to accomplish during my days in Congress. Gila River Indian Community, Arizona.

(© Tami Heilemann)

Me and Jennifer Van der Heide, my chief of staff while I was in Congress and for the first months while at the Department of the Interior. Jennifer was instrumental in the push for my appointment to Interior and the reason for my successes while in Congress. National Christmas Tree Lighting, 2022.

(© Tami Heilemann)

Me just minutes prior to a segment on *The ReidOut* with Joy Reid—one of many on-camera interviews I have given since starting my career. On or around January 13, 2025.

(© Melissa Schwartz)

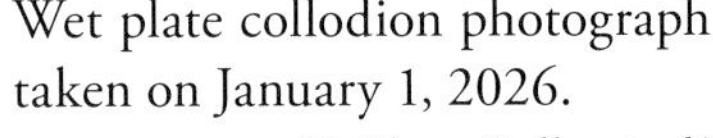

Wet plate collodion photograph taken on January 1, 2026.

(© Shane Balkowitsch)

crats won the five counties in Northern New Mexico, which was something to be proud of.

The Republicans had been shrewd. In 2010, they ran an appealing dark horse gubernatorial candidate in the midst of a Democratic presidency as the country was reeling from an economic disaster caused by Republicans in Washington, DC. It was a perfect storm! After coattail victories under President Obama in 2008 and 2012, the pendulum swung back in a big way in New Mexico in 2014.

The New Mexico Democratic Party's morale was depleted, along with its bank account, so I considered running for state party chair. Many people I trusted told me not to do it, that it was a thankless job, that I would hate it, that my political career would be over before it started. But I knew what our party needed, and I felt I could offer energy and a plan. Anyone will tell you that I never sit around waiting for someone else to act. I work, and I work hard; I saw that our party needed a leader like that. So I traveled the state, talking to Democrats about my vision—to remain united and put in the work to win back our state government.

My sole opponent tried to get me out of the race. He said I could run for vice chair, or that he would make me executive director if I agreed to drop out. Emerge New Mexico had taught me that women often get supporting roles instead of leading ones because we are willing to put in grueling shifts behind the scenes. Flipping that pattern is important: Women are leaders. We have influence, we work hard, and we deserve to be in charge. The strong women in my life taught me that. My simple answer was that he could be *my* vice chair, but I also recognized that people had donated to my campaign for chair, not vice chair or executive director. I told him that I had an obligation to see my campaign through; people were relying on me. So, I continued to make my phone calls and to show up.

The state party chair performs essential functions, leading the ballot qualification processes, running field programs, and carrying out many administrative duties to keep the party viable. In New Mexico, the party chair is elected by local Democratic Party members who serve on the State Central Committee, so the campaign is all about getting most of those four hundred–plus members to vote for you.

My dear friends Scott Tillman and Angie Poss helped immeasurably; together, they were my finance director, my field director, and my communications director. We found volunteers along the way, and I was grateful for all the help I received. I called through the list of State Central Committee members many times. Scott had made a color-coded spreadsheet, and as the months passed, it became greener, row by row, as I convinced party members to support me.

I won the chair's race in the spring of 2015, with 214 State Central Committee votes to my opponent's 168, becoming the first Native woman in the country to be elected state party chair. I promised to be inclusive, to support labor unions, and to ensure the party prioritized the needs of rural communities. My former UNM political science professor Fred Harris had officially nominated me for the post, saying I had a talent for recruiting volunteers that was "better than money." But the party needed money badly. After our wipeout in the recent elections, we were tens of thousands of dollars in debt, and I knew we would need to be on solid financial footing if we were going to move the party forward.

Fundraising was my top priority. In the weeks after my win, Scott would drive to my tribal administration office nearly every day so I could make donor calls from my car in the parking lot during my lunch break. Though we didn't have a lot of money back then, we found enough to throw a celebratory dinner for one of our valued team members when he decided to take another job. I believe it's important to show gratitude for those who have joined the fight for justice, equality, and better lives for our communities; one of the best ways is to share a meal.

For a state party chair, showing up is important. It indicates that you care, and it builds community. I wanted to make sure that every county in the state knew its people mattered to me and that I would step up for our constituents no matter what. I traversed the state with the party's newly elected vice chair, Juan Sanchez, and in many counties and towns, people told us that no state party chair had ever visited. I think that dedication, the thousands of miles I put on my Honda Civic, and the time and energy I invested in the people on the ground helped accomplish our goals. Hard work is much easier if we help each other, and that's the leadership culture I brought to the party.

Juan was a wonderful partner, and together we raised enough money to pull the party out of debt. On a few occasions, we gathered Democrats to celebrate our elected officials. We organized a hearty thank-you event at the Indian Pueblo Cultural Center for state senator Michael Sanchez, then the majority leader. At the time, Sanchez was under constant attack from Governor Martinez, and I wanted to lift him up while creating a sense of fellowship among Democrats. With my own money, I bought a handmade shell bead necklace to honor his service to our state.

About a year after I became party chair, I traveled to the capital of the Navajo Nation in Window Rock, Arizona, about twenty-six miles across the border from Gallup, to attend the sheep butchering portion of the Miss Navajo competition on the Navajo Nation Fairgrounds. While there, I ran into Miss Navajo 1982, Sunny Dooley, who had shown up at one of my campaign events in Gallup several years earlier by accident. She was at the event space concluding other business, and when she saw us unloading the car, she pitched in to help, stayed for the duration of the event, and was a kind and helpful supporter throughout that election year. Her account of competing for the Miss Navajo title nearly thirty years earlier had made me want to witness the competition firsthand.

The pageant requires contestants to master Navajo cultural practices; they must perform these important cultural rites in a full tiered skirt, moccasins, and silver-and-turquoise jewelry, under the watchful eye of an experienced Navajo woman judge. On that day, the women had to start a fire, butcher a sheep, and cook traditional Navajo dishes. With her sheep's back legs tied, each contestant set about respectfully taking its life, then skinning and butchering it—all within the allotted hour. The judge looked stern and took copious notes on each contestant. The crowd watched in silence.

I didn't expect to become emotional during the event, but it was clear that slaughtering the sheep was more than a test of skill with a knife. It displayed a dedication to upholding these young women's traditions, thereby honoring their elders.

During my tenure as state chair, I continued to organize. I often stayed with my friend Bill Monroe in Gallup. On Saturdays, we would set up a canopy and a folding table at the Gallup Flea Market and register voters, and we drove to any number of Navajo Nation chapters to attend meetings and canvass homes. Canvassing used to involve making a list of voters in a community or neighborhood, printing it out, attaching it to a clipboard, knocking on doors, and talking to people about the upcoming election. If you actually talked to a voter on the list, you would indicate whether they planned to vote, for whom, and whether they would vote in person or by mail. These days, there is an app for that.

Gallup is a beautiful southwestern city on Route 66 several miles from the Arizona border. Known as the "Heart of Indian Country," with the Navajo Nation and the Zuni Pueblo in close proximity, it has a deep railroad history and many old buildings, including the El Rancho Hotel, built in 1937 to cater to the movie industry. Hollywood stars like Burt Lancaster and Katharine Hepburn stayed there, and today the hotel has rooms named for that history, like the Marx Brothers and Roy Rogers Suites. I spent a great deal of time in Gallup, both as an organizer and as state chair. Once, while canvassing in a neighborhood there, I couldn't find one of the houses on my walk list. I stopped to ask a few folks working on their roof, and they told me the house I was looking for was a hogan, a traditional Native dwelling built of wood and mud, with a packed-dirt floor. It had been torn down, they said, and the woman who lived there was forced to move. I thought to myself that some progress is really no progress at all.

The 2016 presidential election dominated my time as party chair, and it was transformative, to say the least. The primary pitted former secretary of state Hillary Clinton against longtime Vermont senator Bernie Sanders and opened a schism between so-called establishment Democrats and progressives. When you're a party leader, you must be extra careful not to tip the scales during primary contests. It's part of our responsibility to democracy, to campaign workers, and to the volunteers who fight for their candidates during that process. In 2016, I honed my skills in powering through immense negativity to bring people together.

I knew firsthand what it meant to work for the underdog. In 2008, I volunteered for then-senator Barack Obama during that primary contest. Though I was just getting my feet wet in campaigns, I knew what it meant to work for the guy who wasn't the "establishment" candidate. That's why I gave the same respect to folks who worked tirelessly to elect Sanders as to those who supported Clinton.

Our state party staff comprised four young campaign operatives: Doug Pacheco Myers, Felicia Salazar, Jeff Herrera, and our executive director, Joe Kabourek. They took our commitment to impartiality very seriously. We knew that if a Democrat were going to carry New Mexico in the general election, it would be our job to bring people together after the primary. We did everything we could to welcome new people to the party, holding information sessions about the delegate process, answering phone calls and emails at all hours of the day and night, and welcoming the new energy that Sanders mobilized. On primary day, I took doughnuts from a local shop in Albuquerque to each of the presidential and statewide campaign headquarters. Hillary Clinton won the contest in New Mexico that day, and it seemed likely that she would face the leading Republican candidate, Donald Trump, in November.

Many of us were surprised that Republicans would choose Trump as their nominee, but once they did, we took him as seriously as we would have any opponent. And once his abuse of and disrespect for women, racist rhetoric, and business failures began to percolate, we set out to ensure that our messaging exposed the truth about him. When his son campaigned in San Juan County, we drove to Farmington, hijacked the press corps, and held our own press conference in the pouring rain. We argued that Trump was unqualified to be president and that New Mexico Republicans' failure to hold him accountable proved that Democrats should be in charge.

The primary had been fraught with accusations and, at times, real disdain for the process. Even afterward, when Bernie Sanders came to New Mexico as a Clinton surrogate, a group of his supporters hung signs at an event accusing me and the state Democratic Party of playing favorites in the primary. I was hurt—and even more so when they called for my resignation. It was a serious lesson: No matter your actions or your intentions, there will be people in this world who will try to push their own agenda by any means. But I've never been one to run from adversity. I had a job to do, and I kept doing my job.

After Democrats chose Hillary Clinton as our candidate, I

heard many people say things like "We need a woman president, but not *that* woman." Hillary Clinton was immensely qualified and would have been an experienced, hardworking president, but instead of embracing progress, voters were holding her to a far higher standard than her male opponent. Our country had been led by men for centuries, and most were not nearly as qualified or experienced as Hillary. I found it frustrating but not surprising. In my own small way, I knew what it meant to have to work harder, faster, and longer for a chance at success.

I decided to spend July 4, 2016, in Carlsbad, New Mexico, which was Republican country. I wanted to let the Eddy County Democratic Party chairwoman know I cared about our supporters there, so I went to watch the fireworks with a group of Democrats. We were still waiting for some states to hold their primaries, though across New Mexico, we all were activated to ensure that our state voted blue. On the spur of the moment, Juan decided to join me, so we made the drive together. We stayed late, and it was nearly 10 p.m. by the time we began the four-and-a-half-hour drive back to Albuquerque. Even though I was exhausted from the grueling campaign and the long day, I got behind the wheel, while Juan drifted off to sleep in the passenger seat. Midway through the drive, he awoke to the commotion of me veering off the road and onto the bumpy shoulder. He entreated me to get into the passenger seat. To this day, I am grateful we made it home.

The 2016 Democratic National Convention in Philadelphia was tense. Our delegation was split between Clinton and Sanders supporters, with a modest majority for Hillary. Many of the folks who had come into the party because of their enthusiasm for Sanders had strong opinions about the process and our nominee; I even remember rumors that Sanders could capture the nomination by winning California, a false narrative intended to divide Democrats.

I worked hard to rise above the noise. I remembered all that Brian Colón and his team had done to honor the delegates in 2008, and I tried to do the same. My staff and I pitched in to raise enough money to offer a very substantial breakfast buffet and program each morning, among several other events. I wanted to have a cigar reception, so we loaded up several cases of New Mexico–brewed beer in a car headed to Philly and partnered with a local cigar shop. The reception, in an alley next to the cigar shop downtown, succeeded despite the intraparty bickering.

In September 2016, as the election season reached its climax, I decided to visit Standing Rock, North Dakota, where Native activists were demonstrating against the Dakota Access Pipeline, an oil pipeline more than a thousand miles long that was being laid through their ancestral lands. Activists protested through an organized campout on Standing Rock tribal land. The camp, named Oceti Sakowin, attracted climate advocates and other demonstrators from around the world.

I went to offer my support because I believe the health of our earth and environment are critical for the future of our children and grandchildren. At the tribal building, I connected with Jodi Archambault, a longtime friend, advocate, and former Obama administration staffer, and asked her to put me to work. At the time, they had received thousands of supportive letters, and Jodi gave me the job of helping to log and organize them. I had advocated for letters to be sent from New Mexico tribes and organizations, and I was happy to see them in the stacks I was filing. That evening, I made my way to the camp and cooked green chile stew and tortillas on the campfire. The next day, I rolled out at least one hundred pounds of fry bread dough while others cooked big pots of stew, corn, and beans to feed the protesters.

I saw the NoDAPL protest as the drumbeat for true environmental change heard around the world. Climate change is a reality, and overdependence on finite resources like oil ignores our ability to develop alternative energy for the masses and sets our students and workforce up for failure. Our ancestors protected our land and water, but colonization and assimilation have laid waste to Native lands. I feel called to show up every day and work as hard as I can for future generations because that is what my ancestors did for me.

On Election Night, we hosted an event at the Hotel Andaluz in Albuquerque. Michael Sanchez, our state senate majority leader, lost, but we won back the statehouse, and our statewide offices went solidly blue. We reclaimed the secretary of state's office in part because the Republican incumbent, Dianna Duran, had spent thousands of dollars in campaign funds gambling at casinos and had been jailed for campaign finance fraud.

When national news outlets called New Mexico for Hillary Clinton, everyone in the room cheered, and my phone lit up with congratulatory texts from friends across the country. I was proud of our state, but New Mexico's choice wasn't enough to save our country from a selfish, angry man. Donald Trump won the presidency. I feared for our country and for my child.

I was grateful that Somáh had stayed in Albuquerque for college, where she was paired with a Native American mentor named Monica, who happened to be from Laguna. When Somáh pulled all-nighters to study for midterms, I'd deliver home-cooked food to her dorm. She majored in theater at UNM, and I got to attend all her plays. If she'd gone to college out of state, I would never have been able to afford the travel.

As dawn broke the day after the 2016 election, I felt I had one job: to win back the White House for Democrats in 2020.

CHAPTER 19

A New Voice in Washington

In December 2016, when my term as state Democratic Party chair was nearing an end, Congresswoman Michelle Luján Grisham announced that she was running for governor of New Mexico, opening up the congressional seat in my district. I immediately asked myself if I could run a winning campaign. Could I gather a team I trusted and who trusted me? Could we work hard enough? Could we amass the support and raise the funds needed to run a compelling, relevant, and professional campaign that would touch voters and get them to the polls? My answer to each of these questions was yes, but I gathered a group of my closest friends at my kitchen table over a pan of green chile chicken enchiladas and frijoles to ask them the same questions.

Part of my desire to represent New Mexico stemmed from the fact that a Native American woman had never been elected to the US Congress, something that was about 233 years overdue. Native women had tried, including Ada Deer, who ran to represent Wisconsin's Third Congressional District in 1983, and Diane Benson from Alaska in 2006. During the 2016 election, I helped my friend Denise Juneau run for Congress in Montana, and we thought she would be the first, but she lost to the incumbent Republican. Eventually, we came up with a campaign slogan that seemed to capture the great need for representation among our country's marginalized communities: "Congress Has Never Heard a Voice Like Mine."

I wanted to highlight the missing and murdered Indigenous people crisis, because New Mexico has among the highest rates of missing and murdered Native Americans in the country, and to ensure our military veterans and service members had the support and benefits they needed to prosper. I also wanted to bring national attention to New Mexico's tremendous natural resources, such as sunlight and wind, and their utility in fighting climate change. Renewable energy has long been one of my guiding interests, and I do all I can to walk the talk. For decades, I have worked to contain my own personal carbon footprint by adopting simple daily practices like avoiding single-use plastic bottles and drying my clothes on a clothesline instead of in a dryer. Our environment absorbs so much pollution every day that no one can fix it alone, yet each of us has meaningful choices to make, regardless of how small they may seem. If many people try, we'll make progress together.

I promised myself I'd run an inclusive campaign—both in terms of whom I hired and which voters we targeted—and that I would always work as hard as my staff and volunteers. Bill Monroe, the friend with whom I'd organized in Gallup, had since moved to Northern California, but he came to New Mexico for about six weeks ahead of the primary. He knocked doors, worked the line of moviegoers at the Guild Cinema, and went anywhere else in the First Congressional District where he saw a crowd.

Rachel Joseph, the former chairwoman of the Lone Pine Paiute Tribe in California, also traveled to Albuquerque, by car, to volunteer. Rachel knew what it was like to be a Native woman breaking barriers, and she used her experience and relationships to lift me up because she knew our country would benefit from my perspective. She called hundreds of tribal leaders for me, asking them to support my campaign. And as Rachel made phone call after phone call, I recognized the profound value of Native women's leadership.

When I heard about another Native woman, Sharice Davids, running in Kansas's Third Congressional District, I immediately reached out. One weekend, I went out to Kansas to help with her campaign. We attended a powwow at Haskell Indian Nations University, and found the parking lot full of New Mexico license plates. As I walked through the art market, I greeted many old friends. Indian country is the original "small world," and in this case, I wasn't of great help to Sharice because so many of the people I met in Kansas hailed from our rez community back home and therefore couldn't vote for her. But at least we succeeded in giving her volunteers a boost.

While running for Congress, I attended an annual meeting of the Affiliated Tribes of Northwest Indians in Portland, Oregon. I was on the agenda to speak to tribal leaders and ask for their support. When I stepped down from the dais, a Navajo woman approached and thanked me profusely for the Native American in-state tuition bill I had gotten passed in New Mexico as a law school student. She said it had enabled her brother to attend UNM Medical School. He was the only Native American student in his class.

We ran a grassroots campaign complete with hundreds of volunteers, at least ten of whom worked late the night before the primary in June, punching holes in campaign literature and attaching rubber bands to assemble homemade door hangers because we couldn't afford to have them die-cut. On June 5, 2018, volunteers came to my field office with decorations, food, and extra TVs. We waited in a back room, constantly refreshing the county clerk's Web page, which was not updating as quickly as we wanted. For hours, they posted only early voting results, until finally, the day's votes populated. We had won! My closest opponent was trailing me by 15 percent. The next day, we were ready to implement our general election plan of raising money and getting out votes.

Throughout the month of October, no fewer than fifty volunteers worked in my field office each day. My mom and all my siblings came in to help, and my brother, Judd, and his wife, Daniela, even grabbed a clipboard and canvassed houses for me. The night before the election, I went to the Uptown mall in Albuquerque to look for something to wear. I strolled into White House Black Market and I found a maroon sheath dress with a back zipper and a pearl bead pull—and it was on sale.

On Election Night, my campaign had reserved one of the lounge areas at the Hotel Albuquerque, where the New Mexico Democratic Party held its victory party. When the Associated Press called the race, the room erupted in cheers and applause. Somáh introduced me when I gave my acceptance speech, and my mom joined us onstage.

Later that night, I learned that Sharice Davids had also won and that I would be one of the first *two* Native American women going to Congress. When I had a chance to look at the photos of her victory party, I literally saw myself in her: We were wearing the same dress! Just as I had gone to the mall in Albuquerque, she had gone to her mall in Kansas City. Somewhere along the way, our paths had aligned, and we walked into the same store and bought the same bargain dress. When she and I finally saw each other at our freshman orientation, we laughed heartily about how alike we already were.

Sharice and I became the best of friends. During our first year in Washington, we'd cry every time we were asked to attend House events together and sometimes when we were alone. Knowing that we had nearly a million people in our congressional districts depending on us, along with 574 federally recognized Indian tribes, was deeply moving. We also felt a responsibility to inspire other women from underrepresented communities to run for public office. Whenever we were invited to an unveiling in the Capitol's famous Statuary Hall, or even when we were sitting on the floor of the House listening to our colleagues advocate for a bill, Sharice would lean over and whisper, "Do you believe we get to do this?" We both felt profoundly honored to represent our constituents, but the weight of our ancestors also rested on our shoulders: We knew that in addition to fighting hard for the people in our districts, we needed to make progress for Indian country.

One pressing issue was the epidemic of missing and murdered Indigenous women. As a congresswoman-elect, I attended a US Senate hearing on the subject, and it became clear to me that federal government entities did not have the knowledge or tools to remedy these tragic disappearances and deaths. During my time in Congress, we held panels and hearings on the subject, and I worked to add amendments to the Violence Against Women Act that would benefit Native American women, such as an amendment funding victims' advocates in state courts. We also got a bill signed into law, the Not Invisible Act, that created a commission of victims' families, law enforcement professionals, and survivors of violence and was focused on improving intergovernmental coordination and helping state, tribal, and federal law enforcement allocate resources for survivors and victims' relatives. I must have sounded like a broken record as I reminded my colleagues over and over that the epidemic of missing and murdered Indigenous people and the trafficking of American Indian and Alaska Native peoples had been happening for the past five hundred years. My colleague Ruben Gallego, then chairman of the Natural Resources Subcommittee on Indigenous People, was a strong ally on this and many other injustices affecting Indian country.

Shortly before I was sworn into Congress, the US Commission on Civil Rights had published its Broken Promises Report, a follow-up to a report they had issued fifteen years earlier detailing the federal government's failure over many decades to live up to its responsibilities to Indian country. On December 20, 2018, I wrote an op-ed for the website *The Hill* that called on the United States to live up to its trust and treaty obligations and end the chronic lack of funding for tribes. Shortly afterward, Massachusetts senator Elizabeth Warren called me to say she was ready to do something about the government's long neglect of Indian country, and we agreed to work together. Elizabeth Warren is a true ally to Indian country and has always been a true ally to me. When she commits to a project, she sees it through to the end. She is whip-smart, but so easy to talk to, and she has excellent staff whose values are aligned with hers. Senator Warren understands the struggles of Americans who deserve a fair chance to succeed. Her mentorship helped me more than she will ever know.

Together, we began work on a bill we called the Honoring Promises to Native Nations Act. Both our staffs deserve a tremendous amount of credit and praise for turning our vision into a legislative document. Among other things, the bill would have created an Indian Boarding School Healing Commission, which we eventually extracted as stand-alone legislation. Those bills never passed, but I returned to the issue later as interior secretary.

I was sworn in to my first term in Congress on January 3, 2019, amid a Trump government shutdown. I was proud to be sworn in by the first woman Speaker of the House, Nancy Pelosi. That first term would bring many challenges aside from the chaos and Donald Trump's ethical lapses. We worked and legislated amid Covid-19, racial justice protests, and tremendous cultural upheaval. I kept an even keel and stayed focused on why I was there: to serve the people of New Mexico, help our small businesses, protect our public lands, and stand up for underrepresented communities. But you cannot legislate with your eyes closed. I took a stand on the president's selfish, dangerous behavior and even his tacky lifestyle in the White House. When he told some of my colleagues to go back to where they'd come from, I wrote an op-ed in *The New York Times* saying that Trump lacked the moral authority to tell anyone to leave our country because he himself is not indigenous to this land.

I often felt that it was up to me to fill a void that had existed for centuries. As I welcomed tribal leaders and organizations to my congressional office, I truly felt the power of our ancestors in the rooms with us. I once walked into my office during a workday to find a tribal leader from South Dakota. He was a big man, over six feet tall, with long hair and wearing a suit. He was signing in to our log at the reception desk, and as soon as he saw me, tears flowed from his eyes. We embraced as he told me how grateful he was to me for being there and for the chance to finally meet me. I was always honored by such encounters, and I wanted our office to be a place where all were welcome. I knew how hard advocacy could be, so we invited any activists and others who had come to speak to members of Congress to stop by our offices, rest, refill their water bottles, and leave their bags if they needed to.

One afternoon, the leadership of the National Native American Boarding School Healing Coalition visited my office. This group of Native women is dedicated to getting answers about the federal government's boarding school and assimilation policies that, for a century and a half, tore families apart and sought to destroy Native cultures across the country. Once my office door was closed, coalition member and Native American advocate Deborah Parker spoke. "Can we just sit here for a moment and breathe in the fact that we are in the office of a Native congresswoman?" she asked the group. "We have waited a long time." We did as she suggested, and some of us had tears in our eyes thinking about what it had taken for us to arrive at that moment.

I have often said that I stand on the shoulders of the Native women, men, advocates, and activists who fought for land, water, and fishing rights, as well as health care, education, and housing, long before I was born. The American Indian Movement, for example, was an advocacy group started to help and defend urban Indians from the injustices they faced on the streets of Minneapolis. But those same injustices were happening across the country, to people guilty only of being Indian on the streets of Anytown, USA. At times, it felt as if we were regressing, as if the progress we thought we were making was more like walking in sand.

I was in Congress when George Floyd was murdered by a police officer on the street in Minneapolis—the same city where Native folks had been taken to jail in the trunks of police cars. The Black Lives Matter movement was important to me, I guess because I understood what a history of racism, violence, and poverty meant. I supported any and all legislation that gave people a voice, lifted underrepresented communities, created equity, and mitigated violence. Some of those bills pertained to conserving our public lands, because Mother Earth has suffered greatly throughout our history as well.

I would fly back to Albuquerque nearly every weekend for official and campaign events in my district. Early in my first term, my staff organized a district swearing in for the benefit of my constituents, held at the senior center on Fourth Street NW.

It was a joyous occasion. My mother and Somáh both attended, and we took a photo together and posted it on social media—three generations of my family in one photo.

Had my mother been allowed to remain in the navy after she got pregnant with my oldest sister, I can't help but think that she would have had a successful military career. In Congress, I served on the House Armed Services Committee, or HASC, and I was grateful to have two military fellows join my office and manage my amendments to the National Defense Authorization Act. We worked on several measures that helped remove obstacles for women in the military, and the fellows came up with the idea of a maternity uniform bank for pregnant service members, which we added to the bill. We called it Rent the Camo. I was grateful for my Republican cosponsor; our amendment was bipartisan, and it passed.

As I cast my vote, I thought of my mom. She was in her eighties by then and used a wheelchair. On my weekends home, I'd often drive out to Mesita to cook a week's worth of meals for her. It was nice to spend time together, and she was happy to have home-cooked food while I was away. My nephew Wil visited every day to wash her dishes and make sure she was okay.

Our first in-person town hall at the Albuquerque Museum was packed. I felt so proud to represent a New Mexico district with thoroughly engaged residents who cared about working families, children, and our environment. It was always a pleasure to field questions about issues that we knew would improve the lives of the people I loved. Once, while I was on a telephone town hall, a man came on the phone to ask why I was taking guns away from people, and then he dropped the f-bomb. I instructed my staff to cut him off, not because he disagreed with me, but because my town halls were open to everyone, including my youngest constituents. Thereafter, I warned participants that if they cursed on my telephone town halls, I would hang up.

Those young constituents invited me to their classrooms, visited me in my office, and showed up to ask for my support on various issues, including climate change. One group of children from the Global Warming Express, a group started by elementary school students in Albuquerque, even approached the Albuquerque City Council to ask for a ban on plastic bags and drinking straws. The children were active because they had parents and other adults in their lives who believed in them. I believed in them, too, and always took their questions at my events.

When Joy Harjo was chosen as poet laureate of the United States in 2019, I attended her opening performance at the Library of Congress, where she read some of her poetry and performed with her band. Listening to her poetry set to music moved me to tears, and I was reminded of all the ways art can bring us together.

All my constituents were important to me, and I participated in many committee and subcommittee hearings and organization-sponsored meetings advocating for the rights of transgender people in the military, gay folks in our National Parks, and marriage and adoption equality. Sharice and I sat together on the day in May 2019 when the House passed the Equality Act. The bill would level the playing field for LGBTQ+ Americans by prohibiting discrimination based on sex, sexual orientation, and gender identity, widely expanding the definition of a public accommodation. It would also allow the Justice Department to intervene in federal court on behalf of people who claimed discrimination based on their sexual orientation or gender identity. When the bill passed in the House, we cheered along with visitors in the gallery. Sharice turned to me and asked, as she always did, "Do you believe we get to do this?"

But Republicans would have a different stance on equality for their fellow Americans. It is a shameful truth that we must keep fighting state laws such as bathroom bills, book bans, and "Don't Say Gay" legislation that targets the LGBTQ+ community and seeks to exclude people, negatively influence children, and infringe on the civil rights of so many Americans. The struggle continues, and I am in it for the long haul.

I had won the chairwomanship of the Subcommittee on National Parks, Forests, and Public Lands, and I was vice chair of the House Natural Resources Committee, under the leadership of the esteemed Arizona congressman Raúl Grijalva, God rest his soul. I also stepped up as vice chair of the House Democratic Women's Caucus and cochair of a committee that helped recruit and raise money for women running for Congress. With the 2020 election season close at hand, I wanted to ensure we kept a Democratic House.

Many of us worked hard to help Joe Biden win the 2020 election. When Trump refused to concede his loss, I felt certain that Americans would see the truth and accept the results. But lies can cover a lot of ground before the truth catches up, and we had full-scale denial on our hands. I was sworn in for my second term in Congress amid Covid-19 protocols on January 3, 2021, and three days later, the world changed forever.

No single event has infiltrated my mind quite like the insurrection of January 6, 2021. Sharice and I had decided to walk to work early that day, having no idea what to expect, but thinking it would be best to get there before any crowds arrived. Our offices were one floor apart in the Longworth House Office Building, and once inside, we went our separate ways, agreeing to stay in touch. I had instructed all my staff to work from home that day, but my legislative director, Eric Werwa, was scheduled to get his first Covid-19 vaccine and planned to come in for part of the day. Because of the insurrection at the Capitol, the Longworth garage closed, and Eric was stuck in the office with me for longer than he'd anticipated.

I watched the day's events unfold on the TV screen in my office. My office window faced south, toward C Street, and the Capitol Building was to the north, so I relied on news coverage to see what was happening just across the street. Because of Covid and at the request of Speaker Pelosi, many of us watched the House proceedings from our offices, but as the day wore on and the violence escalated, I worried for my colleagues on the House floor and in the gallery. My phone began to light up with text messages from friends and family back home. "Deb, are you ok?" one friend texted. "All I need is a yes." Who could blame them for being worried? Angry men were busting out windows of the Capitol Building and attacking law enforcement officers with flagpoles at the behest of the president of the United States. Even after the violence against law enforcement officers and the destruction to our nation's Capitol Building, Trump failed to call off the lawlessness.

I called my chief of staff and told her I wanted to record a video showing everyone that I was safe in my office. We posted it to social media. As my legislative director and I waited out the riot behind locked doors, I wondered whether the insurrectionists would discover the maze of tunnels that led from the office buildings to the Capitol, but they seemed focused on destroying our seat of government instead.

At some point late that night, my legislative director was able to get his car out of the garage and drive home. Sharice came downstairs to walk me up to her office, where we joined Representative Kim Schrier of Washington State. Together, we settled in to watch the news coverage, anxiously awaiting our chance to certify the results of the 2020 election. I was immensely disappointed and angry to see some of my fellow members of Congress downplaying the events of that day and taking actions to deny Biden's victory. At some point, Kim mentioned that she had an espresso machine in her office, and we agreed that caffeine was a great idea. We went down to her office, and she made us lattes.

It was after 3 a.m. by the time we voted and began walking toward the exits. I felt dazed and numb that night, but in the coming days, I would learn of, and appreciate, the courage many of my colleagues exhibited during the crisis. While some feared for their lives on the House floor and in the gallery, others worked to comfort and protect them.

Days later, I saw a photo of New Jersey congressman Andy Kim picking up trash early on the morning of January 7 in the

Capitol Rotunda. I believe that in the worst circumstances, it is up to each of us to find a silver lining and focus our energy on what has gone right. But focusing on the positive does not excuse us from calling out the wrongs committed by those in power. We are obligated to do both.

CHAPTER 20

Madam Secretary

After the 2020 election and during the transition, rumors began buzzing through the underground tunnels of the Capitol that President Joe Biden might appoint a Native American to a cabinet position. One day, my chief of staff called to ask whether the group of Native political folks she met with regularly could put my name forward. I reasoned that nothing would come of it. For more than two hundred years, laws and policies had been made for Native Americans, but we were always denied a seat at the table. I told her they could use my name and then went back to work.

Soon after the conversation with my chief of staff, the campaign to nominate the first Native American cabinet secretary began to take on a life of its own. Among the folks interested in achieving Native representation at the highest levels of the federal government was my good friend, the writer, political strategist, and filmmaker Julian Brave NoiseCat, who used his platform at Data for Progress, the think tank where he worked at the time. Julian had put together a cabinet wish list of folks he thought would change our country for the better. My name was added, along with that of Representative Barbara Lee and many others. Julian's hypothetical cabinet had me in good company, to say the least.

Over the next several weeks, relatives, friends, former colleagues, and fellow campaign workers in Indian country and beyond posted and reposted on social media, recorded videos, and sent open letters to President-elect Biden lobbying for my appointment. I was particularly amazed that a group of celebrities, including Cher and a long list of other movie and music stars, signed one of the open letters, people I couldn't imagine knew my name. After that letter circulated on social media, I got text messages from friends asking if I knew Cher, to which the answer was "Of course not!" Mark Ruffalo, who had been a dear friend since my first days in Congress, made a video about my longtime care and regard for the environment that included testimonies from prominent tribal leaders. It was reposted over and over on social media. Even Leonardo DiCaprio expressed his support for my nomination. The organic effort swelled until it became too large to ignore.

As I watched the campaign take shape, I began to realize with all my being why representation truly mattered. In this country's nearly 250-year history, no Native American had served as a cabinet secretary. Since its establishment on Native land, the US government had never included the perspective of an American whose ancestors were in North America long before Europeans began their vast and genocidal colonization. Had I not been elected to Congress, my name might not have been put forth. Through it all, I thanked the ancestors each day for forging a path for me to journey on. I was there because of the sacrifices they had made. I was the beneficiary of their hard work and suffering, and as a result, I was obligated to work for the generations that would come after me and to ensure that even though I was the first, I would not be the last.

In early December, I was summoned to join a video call with President-elect Biden. He sat at his desk, presumably at his home in Delaware, with a member of his transition team at his side. Covid was still keeping us away from the office, and on that day, I was conducting meetings via my laptop from my one-bedroom apartment in Capitol Hill Tower, one of the first apartment buildings in Washington, DC's Navy Yard. I was nervous, of course, and I fidget when I'm nervous, so I sat clasping and unclasping my hands under my glass-topped table.

We talked about our beliefs and how we each saw the job of secretary of the interior. The president-elect was kind and very respectful of what I had brought to Congress, even as he noted that perhaps we would not be perfectly aligned on all issues. As an example, he raised his own differences with Obama years earlier, on marriage equality. I told him I had been working for the Obama campaign as the New Mexico Native vote director at the time and said how pleased I had been to hear of Biden's commitment to defending marriage equality. I stated that we clearly both understood that the environment was a priority, and I thanked him for highlighting the fight against climate change during his campaign. I told him I cared deeply about his initiatives and that I would use my perspective as a Native woman to carry out the mission of the Interior Department and honor his administration's commitments.

After that first conversation, I called a friend who had served as the US ambassador to the UN Human Rights Council to ask what I should say if I got a second call. He said I should first say yes, followed by "It would be an honor to serve." I took notes. When Biden called again to offer me the job, I had a written response ready, because I did not want to risk misspeaking. But the first thing that came out of my mouth was "I don't know what to say, Mr. President-elect," to which Biden said, "Well, you say *yes*!" We both smiled through the phone, and then I successfully read my note aloud: "Yes! It would be an honor to serve our country, Mr. President-elect." Shortly thereafter, at around 3:30 p.m., I received a call from a member of Biden's transition team, who gave me strict instructions not to speak of the appointment to anyone until seven o'clock that evening.

Soon after, Sharice Davids called me on FaceTime to ask if it was true.

"Is what true?" I responded, determined to honor the instructions I had been given.

She said that it was all over social media. I asked her to not tell a soul, and I gave her a play-by-play of the call with Biden. She burst into tears. I was happy to share the news with Sharice first. We had moved Indian country forward as colleagues in the House, we had helped each other win our respective campaigns, and we both recognized the gravity of Biden's decision and its potential ramifications for Indian country. I promised I would never forget why we were there—to right wrongs, to remember where we came from, and to lift up folks who had never seen the stars.

Then the vetting began. I received calls from several staff on the transition team who helped me with security measures for my personal computer and, shortly thereafter, from a lawyer who methodically asked me questions. I did all I could to round up the information they needed. As the Senate confirmation hearings neared, I received more questions from senators on the Energy and Natural Resources Committee. One of them asked for every story I had ever published! I called *New Mexico Magazine*, and they were so helpful in tracking down digital copies of all my articles.

After I was nominated and before my swearing in, I went home to visit my mother, who had worked for decades for the Bureau of Indian Affairs, which is overseen by the Interior Department. My mother's job in the Indian Education Department superintendent's office in Albuquerque required her to travel to Washington, DC, for about a week each year to do a student count. She would count the number of students in schools run by the BIA to make sure each school received enough funding to operate the following year. In Washington, she worked on the fourth floor of the Main Interior Building, known as the MIB; the interior secretary's office was on the sixth floor. One day, she told me, she had seen the door of the secretary's elevator open, and she'd urged her colleague to join her and take the elevator up to the sixth floor so they could meet the secretary. But as soon as the elevator door opened onto the sixth floor, someone there told my mother she couldn't get off. She would have to let the doors close and take the elevator back down. My mother laughed as she recalled her misjudgment, but I sighed. I told her that if she came to visit me in my new office, she could get off the elevator on the sixth floor, and I would welcome her.

On March 18, 2021, I was sworn in as the fifty-fourth secretary of the interior in the ceremonial office of the vice president at the Eisenhower Executive Office Building, directly across the street from the White House. My brother, Judd, had flown to Albuquerque to watch the event streamed on video with our mom. For the swearing in, Somáh held out my dad's Holy Bible, and I placed my hand on it and swore to protect and defend the Constitution of the United States. Afterward, Sharice came to my new office at the MIB, formally known as the Stewart Lee Udall Building. She held my hand and assured me she would be there to support me throughout my tenure.

My new office was grand. It was about the same size as the entire three rooms of my congressional office in the Longworth Building, where at least sixteen people worked on any given day. Completed in 1936, the MIB has oak-paneled walls, murals, a museum, a library, and a store called the Indian Craft Shop; in the building's heyday, there was even an ice-cream parlor on the seventh floor. From there, you can get out on the roof, where on April 8, 2024, many of us gathered to watch the solar eclipse; we also watched the fireworks launched on the National Mall between the Lincoln Memorial and the Washington Monument on Independence Day there. The MIB has the best view of the fireworks, and we always hosted a grateful crowd.

I got to choose art for my office from the collections of the Interior Department Museum and the Bureau of Indian Affairs, which have documented the mission and history of the department since it was created in 1849. While I was secretary, Rick San Nicolas, a master featherworker from Hawaii, gifted the department a gold-feathered cape, which I proudly hung on my office wall.

On my first day as secretary, my sisters and I took the elevator to the fourth floor, where the Bureau of Indian Affairs offices are—the same place my mother worked when she visited Washington. Denise and Zoe quickly befriended one of the employees there, and we were all invited back for a lunch-hour potluck the next day. The invitation reassured me I'd get along just fine there. My sisters made green chile stew, and we returned to the fourth floor the next day at lunchtime.

As we ate, some of the staff told us that they had often seen the secretary's elevator descend and ascend past the fourth floor, but that many secretaries had never stopped there. I vowed to change that. Throughout my tenure, I visited all the department's bureaus and offices, and I visited many of them more than once. I attended staff holiday parties and celebrations when someone retired—I even held some of them in my office. I visited the fourth floor often when tribal leaders arrived for meetings with the Bureau of Indian Affairs assistant secretary. I led in the way I know best—with respect and appreciation for my colleagues. I showed that appreciation in many ways, including by baking New Mexico's traditional biscochitos during the holiday season.

BISCOCHITOS

For the dough:

2 tbsp anise seed

6 cups unbleached flour

2 tsp baking powder

½ tsp salt
1 cup lard
1 cup Crisco
1 cup sugar
3 eggs
½ cup dry white wine

FOR THE COATING:
2 cups sugar
2 tbsp ground cinnamon

Start by pounding the anise seed. I use a mortar and pestle. Mix the flour, baking powder, and salt in a large metal bowl. In a separate bowl, cream the lard and Crisco together along with the sugar, the eggs, and the pounded anise seed. Add the creamed mixture to the dry ingredients and mix gently with a large wooden spoon. When the mixture is cohesive, add the white wine and mix again. You may need to use your hands to fully incorporate the liquid.

Separate the dough into four portions and put into the refrigerator while you gather your other supplies. You will need at least two baking sheets, a rolling pin, flour for rolling out the dough, a cookie cutter, and a 9x13-inch pan in which to mix the coating.

Preheat the oven to 350°F. Roll the first portion of dough to ¼-inch thickness and cut with a cookie cutter—I use a fluted cutter that is about 3 inches across. Transfer the cookies to a sheet pan. Bake for about 10 minutes. You can bake two pans of cookies at once, switching positions in the oven about halfway through. Meanwhile, mix together the sugar and cinnamon.

When the bottoms of the cookies are slightly browned, remove from oven and transfer to a cooling rack or waxed paper. Roll more dough and put more cookies into the oven. Coat the baked cookies thoroughly with the cinnamon sugar.

I immediately set out to learn all I could about the work of the Interior Department. My very first act was to host a department-wide video conference. I felt it was important for all the career staff and appointees to actually see me, even if I was just a face on their computer screen. While in Congress, I had seen some of the negative changes implemented by the first Trump administration, such as moving the Bureau of Land Management headquarters to Grand Junction, Colorado, thousands of miles from its longtime address on C Street NW in Washington. This increased uncertainty and harmed morale, which caused many career staff to quit, diminishing the bureau's effectiveness. My colleagues and I in Congress had used our oversight power to question Interior Department appointees in committee hearings, but our efforts did not always lead to the changes we sought, and the harm caused by some of their actions and policies persisted.

I felt certain that if we were to accomplish the Biden administration's goals, we would need a staff that could embrace their work, so improving the morale of the department's more than 65,000 employees in nearly every state across the country became a personal goal. I made it a priority to thank staffers whenever I had the opportunity, and I worked at getting to know the public servants who dedicated their careers to the department. They were the people I relied on to make progress on clean energy, climate resilience, and landscape restoration and to help the United States live up to its trust and treaty obligations to our Indian tribes.

That August, I married my longtime partner Lloyd Sayre, whom everyone calls Skip. A progressive Democrat from the Bay Area, Skip had carried petitions in California supporting the presidential run of my former political science professor and dear friend and mentor Fred Harris. Skip and I hit it off immediately, and he had supported me through all my political campaigns, even coming to my campaign office in 2012 to work the phone bank on my behalf. After several years together, we felt it was time to make our relationship official.

The Boston Marathon is normally held on Patriots' Day, the third Monday in April. But in 2021, because of Covid, it was held on Indigenous Peoples' Day, in October. I was pleased that the organizers chose to highlight Indigenous runners, considering that "Heartbreak Hill," the grueling hill at mile twenty, had been named for Narragansett elite runner Ellison "Tarzan" Brown. Brown's top competitor in the 1936 marathon, John Kelley, passed him on the hill at mile twenty and tapped him on the back, perhaps goading Brown into running faster and ultimately winning the race. A reporter captured that sequence in a story, dubbing the place where Kelley lost Heartbreak Hill.

Race organizers called my office to ask if I would come to Boston to give a speech at an event to celebrate Indigenous runners who had taken part in the Boston Marathon. I was thrilled to be asked. I had read about Mi'kmaq runner Patti Catalano Dillon, and the organizers said she would be there. After a few calls back and forth, my staff informed me that the race director had also invited me to run the marathon. Normally, contenders must have a qualifying time to enter the race, and I didn't have a recent marathon time that would have qualified me, so I was overwhelmed with gratitude.

The prerace event attracted runners and supporters alike. Life-size photo banners of Tarzan Brown and Patti Dillon adorned the stage. At one time, the Boston Marathon had barred women from competing. In 1966, Roberta "Bobbi" Gibb became the first when, in shorts and a hoodie, she hid in the bushes near the start of the race and began running with the men. I was thrilled to meet Joan Benoit Samuelson, the Olympic medalist whose career and book had so inspired me years earlier. I got to tell her how much her guidance had meant to me and to convey my appreciation for the example she'd given women runners around the world. I also got to meet Patti Dillon on the eve of the race, and she offered the best advice: "Don't go out too fast." The marathon start at Hopkinton is downhill, and it's easy to overuse that momentum.

Boston was the first marathon for which I trained with a security detail. My detail as secretary comprised nearly a dozen members who worked various shifts, and the Saturday crew consistently ran or bicycled alongside me during my long runs. Every morning on weekdays, they would join me at my residence, and we would run the four miles to my office, turning right at the US Capitol and down the National Mall to Eighteenth and

C Streets. Sometimes I could stretch my morning runs to five miles by running up the steps and around the back of the Lincoln Memorial, passing the place of honor where Reverend Martin Luther King Jr. gave his "I Have a Dream" speech.

The National Mall is peaceful in the early mornings, and it felt surreal to run on ground that memorializes so much of American history in one place. The Capitol Building itself is majestic, its cast-iron dome and marble steps connoting the important work that should take place within its walls. As for the World War II Memorial, every time I passed its bronze wreaths, which recognize the sacrifices made by each of our states to fight fascism and protect democracies around the world, it made me think of veterans, including those in my family. During cherry blossom season, the mature trees—gifts from Japan—festoon the Mall with bursts of color. Each year that I was secretary, I sounded the starting horn and ran the Cherry Blossom ten-mile race.

I balanced my Boston Marathon training with a hectic travel schedule, and my security detail grew practiced at scoping out places to run near our hotels; in a pinch, I would use the treadmills at hotel fitness centers. I got my miles any way I could.

On race day, my security detail drove me almost to the starting line. The race has rolling starts, meaning that after the elite runners take off, other contenders can just start running; there are no time corrals. One member of my security detail ran with me, while another rode a bicycle. My goal was to finish in under five hours.

We approached the starting line about ten minutes after

the gun went off and the elite runners bolted. I remembered Patti Dillon's advice, *Don't go out too fast*, and I tried to restrain myself as I started running downhill. It was a high-energy race, meaning that the spectators truly treated the marathon as a holiday worth celebrating. Families brought lawn chairs out to their front yards and picnicked along the route, and children and adults alike held up encouraging signs. At one place along the course, an organization had set up mini trampolines and kids bobbed up and down in celebration. Several hundred yards from Wellesley College, we heard a roar. As we ran past, it seemed that every single Wellesley student was out on the lawn holding up homemade signs and cheering, shouting, and cajoling us on.

At some point, I found myself in a portion of the course that was lined with trees. It was magical running over orange, yellow, and soft red leaves that spun and danced with each footfall. I crossed the tape and received my medal less than two minutes under my goal time.

While in Congress, I'd championed the target set by many conservation organizations that if we preserved 30 percent of our lands and 30 percent of our waters, we would be on the right track with respect to the climate crisis. I was even part of a global effort known as 30x30, having joined its steering committee and successfully advocated to get this goal included in the DNC's 2020 platform. During my four years at the Interior Department, I was proud of the team we assembled to move the clean energy transition forward, whose members diligently stewarded our public lands and embraced our responsibility to abide by the laws set down in the Endangered Species Act.

The landmark Bipartisan Infrastructure Law and the Inflation Reduction Act signed by President Biden allowed our department to ensure that Indian tribes received funding for climate resilience, that we could heal the open wounds cut into the earth by extractive industries, and that natural landscapes, from grasslands to salt marshes, became a focus of our responsibility to future generations.

Healing our earth's wounds was important, but so was tending the wounds US policy had inflicted on Native people. I was working on an op-ed about the legacy of Indian Boarding Schools when news broke that the remains of more than two hundred children had been found in a mass grave on the grounds of the Kamloops Indian Residential School in Canada. After several edits back and forth with *The Washington Post*, my piece went to print. In it, I wrote about my own family and how abusive boarding schools had shaped my grandparents' lives. "We have a generation of lost or injured children who are now the lost or injured aunts, uncles, parents and grandparents of those who live today," I wrote. "Though it is uncomfortable to learn that the country you love is capable of committing such acts, the first step to justice is acknowledging these painful truths and gaining a full understanding of their impacts so that we can unravel the threads of trauma and injustice that linger."

Soon after, we announced the Federal Indian Boarding School Initiative, a comprehensive effort to recognize the troubled legacy of federal policies designed to separate children from their families and communities in order to "Americanize" them. We wanted to address the intergenerational impacts of such policies and shed light on the trauma they inflicted on victims and their descendants.

Once the first report was completed, I knew we needed to give voice to the survivors and descendants of that shameful period of our country's history, so we embarked on a listening tour, called the Road to Healing. In more than a dozen locations across the country, we heard from mothers who had not told their children what they endured at Indian Boarding Schools until the day they testified. We heard from men who conveyed in painful detail how they had been beaten and why. We heard from people who had had their languages and cultures stolen from them. At the same time, the tribes who hosted us shared their traditions, with singing, dancing, prayers, and even color guards in vibrant ceremonial outfits, proud evidence of their service to our country.

The listening tour uncovered more questions, so we drafted a second report that included greater detail about the schools named in the initial report and the funding that had fueled them over more than a century. We also researched the school cemeteries—where they were, how long they had been there, and how many children had been interred. The second report included a list of recommendations, one of which was that the government should issue a formal apology to Indian country for the misguided effort that had brought despair on nearly the entire Indigenous population of the United States. I will never forget the woman who described in her testimony the silence that descended upon her traditional village after all the children had been taken away to boarding school. When I think about my ancestors, I am humbled by the fact that they survived at all.

After we released the second report, the White House called to say that President Biden wanted to issue an official apology, and on a sunny October day on the ancestral homelands of the Gila River Indian community, near Phoenix, the president brought his whole heart to bear, noting that the apology was "long overdue." "Generations of native children [were] stolen, taken away to places they didn't know, with people they'd never met who spoke a language they had never heard," he said. "It's horribly, horribly wrong. It's a sin on our soul."

It was somewhat surreal that the hard work we had done to bring this painful chapter of American history to light actually resulted in an admission by the US government that it had caused pain, death, and the destruction of Indigenous languages and cultures. As I listened, a burden seemed to lift from my shoulders. Under the wide, blue, cloudless sky, I believe President Biden felt our gratitude for the heartfelt apology that Indian country had so long been denied. It served as a culmination of the work we had done to live up to our promises.

I visited hundreds of places as secretary of the interior. Many of the lands the department manages are sacred to the Indian tribes that live and work nearby. In some cases, Native Americans were essentially kicked off their ancestral homelands to make way for a National Park or National Wildlife Refuge. Regardless of who has the title, Native people still consider these lands sacred and continue to care for them. In that spirit, I always thanked the federal civil servants who had dedicated their careers to reviving an ecosystem, researching and writing of a place that needed protection, or even ensuring that a trail was safe to hike. Whether I was hundreds of feet below the earth's surface and in awe of Wind Cave National Park, in South Dakota, or along the banks of a salmon-rich river in Alaska, I recognized that those lands were desired by the federal government because they had been stewarded so lovingly by the ancestors. As the first Native American cabinet secretary in US history, I strived to ensure I showed up each day as a Pueblo woman first. That is my identity. Pueblo people are farmers, builders, runners, and fierce protectors of our culture and traditions, and throughout my tenure, I learned that people across our country share my values. These values are what unite us in the work that sustains the wild places we all love.

The last footrace I ran as secretary was the Canyon de Chelly Ultra in northeastern Arizona in 2024, where I had hiked with Somáh years earlier. Spider Rock is a prominent formation there, standing about eight hundred feet tall, and the canyon walls are towering sandstone cliffs. I learned about the ultramarathon from our tour guide while visiting the canyon on an official Interior Department trip. As soon as we returned to our vehicle after the tour, I told my colleagues, "We are running that race."

That night at my hotel, I looked up the race and set a calendar reminder to register when the lottery opened. On that day, race director Shaun Martin prints all the entrants' names and puts them in a big stewpot. His family helps him film the event and post it to social media, so prospective runners know whether they've been selected in the first round. When my name was chosen randomly from the pot, Somáh got a text from a friend asking if I was running the Ultra. That's how I found out I needed to begin training for a thirty-four-mile race in Canyon de Chelly.

I decided that my longest training run would be twenty-six miles, and I set out to conquer that distance. My last year as secretary was busy with travel, but I ran at every opportunity. In Maine, I ran eight miles, and in New Mexico, fourteen. On the day we planned a twenty-mile run, I was in Washington, DC, and two members of my security detail accompanied me—one running with me and one in a vehicle, meeting us at various crossroads. We were also joined by three senior officers of the US Park Police, two of whom planned to run the race. It rained the entire day. Our course traversed many DC-area trails and passed the Washington National Airport. By mile eighteen, I was ready to walk. I didn't end up completing a twenty-six-mile training run for the Ultra, but, for some reason, when I got to Chinle, Arizona, I wasn't worried about finishing.

The Canyon de Chelly Ultra was organized and managed almost entirely by Shaun Martin's family. The prerace meeting on the eve of the event detailed the race's history and gave us a sense of the sacredness of the canyon and the power of nature. Shaun talked about how, in some past races, water from the snowmelt ran deep; on this race day, he said, the soft sand would present a challenge to even the most seasoned runners. I left the meeting inspired. The following morning, Shaun's father gave a blessing before the race started, while his mother and other relatives cooked mutton and corn stew, beans, and fry bread for those who crossed the finish line. Shaun's nephews, brothers, cousins, and many other volunteers ran the aid stations.

We all set out at the starting bell; the race would last for eleven hours. At about mile sixteen, we began to climb a trail to the halfway point, which is at the rim of the canyon. I had to reach mile seventeen by noon to stay in the race. Along the way, we checked in with volunteers at each aid station; their purpose was to ensure that runners finished in the allotted time. Each runner needed to reach each aid station in time to arrive at the finish line before 6 p.m. When the race started, I was sure I would finish in time, but by mile seventeen, I found myself working hard to beat the clock.

I reached the halfway point a few minutes after noon, and the volunteers at the top aid station logged us as arriving on time. I sat down to change my socks and drink a Coke before beginning my descent, peanut butter and honey sandwich and bag of potato chips in hand. The day before the race, Judd, a serious runner himself, had advised me to keep my calorie count up, and I ate all I could at every aid station. He also said I needed to drink more water, soda, or electrolyte drinks than I thought I needed. I refilled my CamelBak hydration pack at least three times during the race and drank extra along the way.

In the last five miles, I stepped up my pace and continually asked my running mates how much time we had left. A sense of elation came over me when I glimpsed the finish line. I had felt certain I would be the last runner to crawl across, but I came in 110th out of 126 finishers. I have never been so happy to sit down and enjoy stew and fry bread as I was that day. I awoke the next morning expecting the worst, but thanks to the ocean of soft sand along the bottom of the canyon, my joints had suffered minimal stress, and I felt refreshed.

Had I not visited Canyon de Chelly on an official trip, I

might not have known about the race. Spending nearly eleven hours on foot in the canyon had been an unforgettable gift.

I am often asked about my most memorable experience while serving as interior secretary. To name a favorite would be like choosing one's favorite child, but before the fall of 2022, I had never in my life excavated a sea turtle nest or helped baby turtles to the ocean. That changed on an official trip to the US Virgin Islands in November 2022, one of many visits to places where the Interior Department had a bureau or office that fulfilled our mission in some way. In the Virgin Islands, National Park and National Wildlife Refuge units were under the department's management, so we planned a trip there to bring attention to their needs and successes.

One of those places was the Sandy Point National Wildlife Refuge on the island of Saint Croix. First, the staff gave us an overview of the area and the projects of the refuge. Then we walked along a short trail from the parking lot to a wide, golden sandy beach; it was a gloriously sunny day. The turtle scientist explained that a mother turtle can lay more than sixty eggs per nest. Most of those eggs will hatch all at once, and the baby turtles climb up using one another as step stools to reach the surface of the beach. Propelled by instinct, they crawl toward the ocean, leaving their tracks in the sand. The scientist said she had walked the beach at 5 a.m. that day to mark the turtle tracks so that after the beach closed for the day, she could return to help any remaining young reach the water.

We came upon a marked nest, and the scientist instructed me to begin digging gently with my hands. As I did, I uncovered eight or ten baby turtles crawling around, unable to ascend because there were too few of them to use one another as leverage. We carefully removed the turtles from the nest and placed them in a bucket. We inventoried each hatched egg, each egg that had not hatched, and the number of live and healthy hatchlings. The Wildlife Refuge staff told me to hold them "like a little hamburger," so I grasped one gently between my thumb and two fingers. Its turtle arms and legs paddled the air, as if it were practicing for the ocean.

Once the nest was fully excavated, we replaced the sand, approached the waves, and loosed the turtles. They hurried toward the surf, and we stood onshore, our bare feet in the cool water, crying as if saying goodbye to dear friends. That day we learned that out of every one thousand sea turtles that hatch, only one will grow to maturity. Climate change makes the life cycle of sea turtles more difficult as time goes on. Sea level rise and warming oceans challenge their habitats, along with those of nearly every species on earth.

A trip to the Okefenokee National Wildlife Refuge, in southern Georgia, elicited a similar emotional response. Its 450,000 acres of unspoiled swampland are home to a plethora of birds, aquatic animals, and a healthy peat layer that supports a complex and critical ecosystem. Trail Ridge borders the swamp on the east and, like the lip of a glass, acts as a barrier to the hydrology inside the swamp. In the name of progress, early capitalists tried to literally drain the swamp by digging a canal that would connect it to a nearby river; thankfully, the effort failed. The canal still exists, and we used it to tour the swamp and see what a healthy peat ecosystem looks and feels like. At one point, my colleague and assistant secretary for fish and wildlife and parks,

Shannon Estenoz, got out of the boat and stepped onto a patch of peat to demonstrate its sponginess.

I hadn't been to a swamp since my dad took my siblings and me to the Great Dismal Swamp in Virginia when I was about seven years old. Both places have "blackwater," meaning the water is darkened by leaves and other decomposing organic matter. I find blackwater startlingly reflective—like a mirror that can reveal the benefits of good land stewardship. That day in the depths of the Okefenokee, I saw alligators, egrets, and gauzy-textured moss hanging from the trees like a best friend. I felt a deep appreciation for my childhood voyage to the Dismal Swamp, where each time my dad's oars hit the water, they propelled us toward the future he wished for us all.

The trip to Okefenokee was one of many occasions during my tenure in the House and the Interior Department when I wished my parents could have joined me. Another was during my time in Congress, when then-chairman of the Joint Chiefs of Staff General Mark Milley invited me and several of my colleagues on the House Armed Services Committee to breakfast at the Pentagon. That was an occasion when I would have called my dad to announce where and with whom I had breakfast. Or when the commandant of the Marine Corps invited me to the Marine Barracks to attend a sunset parade held in my honor. I invited my brother, and when my security detail dropped us off at Commandant David H. Berger's front door, we stepped onto a red carpet and were greeted by the commandant himself. I turned to look at Judd and saw that he had tears in his eyes. So did I. We both were thinking about our dad. My father passed away in 2005, and my mother in 2021. I guess those feelings surfaced because I had always strived to make my parents proud. Perhaps in those moments, they would have been.

I was thinking of my mother when, on one of my last days as secretary, I asked my staff to help me schedule an open house so everyone in the building would have a chance to see the secretary's office. There was a line down the sixth-floor hall that day, and I welcomed each of my colleagues for a photo in front of the fireplace, where a portrait of Hunkpapa Lakota chief Gall hung above the mantel.

CHAPTER 21

Leading Fiercely

"Running for office is not for the faint of heart," I heard Speaker Nancy Pelosi say many times. Especially when addressing women candidates, she would tell us, "You have to know your *why*."

When I returned to Albuquerque that chilly January day in 2025, I knew my why. I was fired up to defend my beautiful state against the chaos and cruelty of the second Trump administration, so I spoke to friends about my intention to run for governor of New Mexico. I jumped into the fight against Trump's ignorance about climate change, his cuts to the Veterans Administration, his tax giveaways for billionaires, and his evisceration of Medicaid and SNAP—programs that had helped me and thousands of other New Mexicans raise our children. The general dismantling of our federal government seemed imminent, and I would not sit by and watch it happen. If the choice was between a quiet life behind the scenes and methodically talking to as many voters as possible in New Mexico over the course of eighteen months in the hope of bringing them a better future, I would choose the latter every time.

We launched our campaign on February 11, 2025, and my why grew clearer. As I traveled the state on our nineteen-stop launch tour, I heard from New Mexicans who wanted to help determine the direction of our state and our country. They told me they wanted to be listened to. In response, I decided to be up front about the challenges we faced and my desire to address them collectively. I would never be so self-centered as to believe that only my thoughts or acts mattered.

I refer to myself as a thirty-fifth-generation New Mexican. My connections to the land are undeniable, but so, too, are those of many across our state whose families have been here for centuries. Sharing time with them makes me feel right at home.

One Friday on the campaign trail, I had the profound joy of meeting with members of the New Mexico Acequia Association, in Mora County on the banks of Morphy Lake. Acequias are ancient irrigation systems that are stewarded by communities across New Mexico. Morphy Lake is in a state park, but the land is owned and stewarded by the Acequia Association. Pine trees abound there, bringing beauty and shade, but the area beyond the lakeshore was badly damaged by the Calf Canyon/Hermits Peak Fire of 2022, and people now refer to it as the "burn scar area." As we drove to the lake, the landscape resembled burned matchsticks uniformly arranged up and down hillsides. We also saw scrub oak and grasses—evidence of new forest growth that gave me hope.

We arrived at a picnic area by the lake, where folding tables had been neatly arranged in rows and set for lunch. There were two pots of red chile beans and bags of Fritos on serving tables nearby. Frito pies: a handful of Fritos covered with a ladle of red chile beans, followed by lettuce, tomatoes, and shredded cheddar cheese. It's a crowd favorite. Before eating, Dabi Soledad García, who uses music, poetry, prayer, and ritual to uphold New Mexico culture, led us in a song they had written about acequias.

RED CHILE BEANS FOR FRITO PIES

2 cups dry pinto beans, washed and soaked overnight
½ medium yellow onion, diced
2 tsp Crisco or manteca
1 pound ground beef
1 garlic clove, minced
Salt to taste
2 tbsp red chile powder
1½ cups pureed red chile
Dash of dried oregano

In a 4-quart pot, bring 2 quarts of water to a boil on high heat, add the soaked beans, and reduce to a simmer for about two and a half hours. (You may also use a slow cooker.) Add ¼ cup of the onion and the Crisco or manteca. Simmer for at least another hour or two. Try not to stir the beans too much while they cook.

When the beans are tender but not mushy, fry the ground beef in a large skillet over medium heat. When it is almost done, drain the grease, add the remaining onion and the garlic, and continue to cook until onions are transparent and soft. Add the salt and chile powder and cook several more minutes. Add the pureed red chile and the oregano and increase the heat to medium high. When bubbles form, stir and reduce the heat. Simmer for 15 minutes, stirring occasionally.

When the beans are fully cooked, add to the beef mixture and serve with corn bread or warm tortillas, or make into Frito pies.

A few people spoke during the lunch, including a teenage girl from Las Vegas, New Mexico, who had landed a position on the Acequia Youth Conservation Corps. At the time, she was the only girl in the small group of young people who physically worked to maintain the acequias in the area. She approached the front of the group dressed in a baseball cap, blue jeans, and worn work boots. She smiled as she talked, speaking fondly about growing up near the Gallinas River and how it connects New Mexico's communities. Hearing her speak that way about her conservation work gave me hope for our future.

Nearly every day on the campaign trail, I meet people who are scared and worried about our democracy. Sometimes I feel like a counselor helping people weather an emotional storm. I mention to those in distress that our country has been through many eras of turmoil, and we have always survived. I don't always say this, but I believe that worrying is unproductive and that only concerted action will help us focus on the bright future we all want for our children. My campaign gives supporters ideas for op-eds to submit to local papers, and I encourage people to call our federal delegation offices and let them know we appreciate their efforts to resist cuts to Medicaid and the VA and to speak out against the administration's inhumanity toward people who are in our country without official permission. I tell them that we must win back the House to rein in the chaos.

In the 2024 election, New Mexico Democrats lost 3 percent of voters to the Trump campaign. I believe that if we want to win elections, we must listen more than we talk. In a way, I am returning to my roots as an organizer. I am meeting voters where they are in their own communities, not mine, traveling to underrepresented villages, towns, and neighborhoods and showing up to hear what they have to say. It sounds too simple to be true, but I believe government must care for those it serves.

On this day, writing at the kitchen table, I feel like I'm back where I started. Skip and I divorced in 2025, after I realized that I enjoy being alone too much to compromise my independence and that I want to devote my remaining years to finding solutions to some of our biggest problems and making people's lives better. I didn't get the job I wanted after my federal service because of the chaotic political climate. Many New Mexicans tell me they are working hard but can't earn enough money to support themselves and their families. I empathize when I hear these stories because I know what it's like to have one dollar in your bank account and a hungry kid to feed.

The injustices of our era sometimes feel too heavy to bear, but this moment does not define us. We are defined by those who came before us, who worked and sacrificed, who put themselves in harm's way to defend us and our planet. It's time to embrace that power.

EPILOGUE

Marathons

When I started running, each time was a trial. Since then, I have run hundreds of miles on paved roads and dirt trails. I love the crunch of gravel or the bounce of pine needles under my feet, inhaling deeply beneath grand redwood trees or powering up a service road to get to the top of some hill so I can take in the view. While running on the Anacostia Trail in Washington, DC, I have been blessed to see deer, bald eagles, and wild turkeys. At the same time, and each time I ran along the Anacostia River, I thought about what the region used to be, immense swampland, and how the ancestors lived and prospered there. It may be difficult for some folks to imagine, but the nation's capital was home to communities of Indigenous Anacostan, Piscataway, and Pamunkey people fishing, hunting, and thriving.

In addition to running, I have crewed for others. Twice, I crewed on the 135-mile Badwater Ultramarathon, a footrace that begins in Death Valley, at the lowest elevation in the United States, and ends at the Portal Road on Mount Whitney, eight thousand feet above sea level. On both occasions, my runners reached the finish line after midnight, and I found myself enveloped by inky blackness beneath a sky full of stars. I am not often at a loss for words, but being surrounded by the darkest sky I have ever experienced challenged my thinking. No longer was I an inconsequential speck of earthly matter, but part of the universe. I believe that if everyone had such experiences, we would all feel an urgent devotion to our planet.

Running is an ancient tradition, and to me, it is not so much a hobby as an obligation. My ancestors sacrificed comfort, endured hardship, and survived in an immense desert so I could be here. I am grateful for my physical ability to run and for Creator's gift of good health. I believe I must share this gift any way I can. My running days are not over; I hope to stay on the trails for many more years. I've always dreamed of running the Badwater Ultramarathon myself, and even though the days have passed into years and my obligations to serve my communities continue, perhaps I will train for that race someday. For now, I find daily joy in putting one foot in front of the other.

If you've read this book from the beginning, you can see that I am not like a lot of politicians. I do not come from people who were born into the political echelons of our country. I didn't graduate from an Ivy League school. I didn't even start college until I was twenty-eight. Neither of my parents graduated from college; they were humble public servants who devoted themselves to sustaining our communities and our country. Their sense of duty has been my North Star. And that's the point, isn't it? People with real, lived experience should have opportunities to serve. Elections should never be about the candidate, but about the people that candidate strives to represent.

After serving my state as a congresswoman and traveling thousands of miles to the farthest edges of our country as a cabinet secretary, there are still days when I marvel at the beauty of New Mexico. When the sun sets behind a mountain range, painting the sky in rich oranges and reds, or when I'm running in the foothills of the Sandia Mountains, I feel deeply grateful. That gratitude compels me to safeguard our culture and history, to protect what we have built over centuries, and to pass it on to future generations.

Everyone has something to offer. Whether you live in an Indian pueblo, a small town, or a big city, your voice matters in our politics. I think often of a woman I met in a remote Indian pueblo community here in New Mexico in 2012. There was no Native American community in New Mexico I did not visit that year, and one chilly October day, that young woman stood inside her house, and I on the front porch, with a screen door separating us, for no less than twenty minutes. As four children of varying ages came and went, looking up at me and listening to our conversation before returning to their play, the woman asked many questions about my candidate: Where did Obama stand on health care and the economy? Did he know that Indian tribes in New Mexico needed housing? Did he care about Head Start for her young children?

Twenty minutes is a lifetime to an organizer whose voter contact goals consistently increase as the campaign goes on, yet I knew I needed to stay, even to the detriment of the spreadsheet I'd turn in to my field director that night. Here was a young mother, maybe in her late twenties, who was making time to speak with a person she had never met because she wanted to know more about my candidate and how national politics would affect her life and the lives of her children. I was on her time.

Every election year, we ask people to get out and vote for candidates who share our values, sometimes without thinking hard enough about the lives those voters lead. As volunteers and organizers, perhaps we need to take a step back and think about them. How many jobs do they have, and how extensive are their responsibilities at home? Are they caring for children and parents in equal measure? What are their hopes and dreams? Their struggles? What would actually make their lives better? If we took the time to listen, perhaps we could begin uniting people toward a common purpose and changing our country into the place it was meant to be: a nation that values irreplaceable things such as health, community, equal justice, land, air, and water above all else.

Folks try to categorize us as establishment Democrats, liberal Democrats, progressives, blue dog, yellow dog, and every other "type" of Democrat you care to name. I am a Democrat because I believe in the values I was raised with: Commitment to my community. Helping those in need. Always being cognizant of how my actions impact others and the environment. Kindness. Putting the well-being of children ahead of my own. I believe I have an obligation to help elect candidates who share these values because I want a better world for the people I love.

It is up to me, and it is up to you, to return to the values handed down to us by previous generations and to lead by example. Practicing the politics of community means acknowledging that we are part of something bigger than ourselves. That can be the starting point.

ACKNOWLEDGMENTS

This book was a notion long before I ever put fingers to keys. When I had the idea to begin writing, my friend and continual colleague Felicia Salazar encouraged me. She would come to my apartment on Saturdays to help flesh out ideas, and she later brought me her edits on paper. Without her initial support, I might well have set the idea aside and never picked it up again. Thank you, Felicia, for your amazing editing skills, your brilliant writing, and your keen political sense.

When Somáh was nine years old, she eulogized my dad, her grandfather, at his funeral, from a piece she had written and edited on her own. Since then, Somáh's writing has flourished, and I am grateful for the many hours they spent with me on video conference, plodding through some of the most difficult stories I wanted to tell, one word at a time. Thank you so much for your love, decisiveness, and splendid use of adjectives.

I also wish to thank my sisters and mentors, Zoe and Denise, for dropping what they were doing to read this manuscript in its entirety and then reminiscing with me on the phone for hours, comparing notes about childhood memories. I want to thank my brother, Judd, for always having my back. I sincerely appreciate Sharice Davids for being like a sister to me, along with all my Pueblo sisters who have been there for me the longest.

I thank Brendan Jackson, who read many parts of this book and offered excellent feedback while pushing me to be more descriptive and dig deeper.

My thanks to Skip Sayre for his immense and valuable support throughout my runs for lieutenant governor, Democratic state party chair, Congress, and beyond. His help and marketing prowess were critical to my campaigns.

Deepest gratitude to David Dunaway, my college English professor, who originally inspired me to write in earnest. His instruction, critiques, work ethic, and edits to this book have made me want to be a better writer and a better person.

I thank my agent, Gail Ross, and everyone at William Morris Endeavor for their trust, their professionalism, their kindness, and their support. Long before Gail even knew I could write, she was willing to help me see my vision through.

Thank you to Serena Jones, Zoë Affron, and everyone at Henry Holt and Company for their patience, trust, and great teamwork.

A gigantic thank-you to my amazing editor, Vanessa Gezari, who met me online one day and flew out to Albuquerque the next to help me get my book organized. I am grateful for her insight about the world and how it applied to my stories. Her attention to detail and chronology made my book what it was truly meant to be.

For my parents, God rest their souls, who always did their

best and taught me and my siblings all the important things and to love one another.

Throughout my years as a public servant, I have had many opportunities to meet Indigenous people in the United States and around the world. There is one characteristic all of us share: We have an immense belief that we are all connected by the earth and the power of our ancestors. Throughout my time as congresswoman and secretary of the interior, Indigenous people have told me that they pray for me. Those prayers have helped me find solace in difficult times, muster courage when I have needed it, and seek the wisdom to help. I am grateful beyond words for their generosity and our connection, no matter on whose ancestral land I am standing or what challenge I am facing.

Finally, I wish to acknowledge the many generations of ancestors across Indian country whose shoulders have always been there for me to stand on. They passed down the lessons we all need to shape a better world.

ABOUT THE AUTHOR

Deb Haaland, a thirty-fifth-generation New Mexican, organized for President Obama, led the New Mexico State Democratic Party to victory, and became one of the first Native women to serve in the US House of Representatives. She also made history as the first Native American appointed to a US president's cabinet. A military kid, a single mom, and a Pueblo woman, Haaland has championed working families, fought to give underserved communities a voice, and taken action to address the climate crisis. She lives in Albuquerque, New Mexico.